Catholic Church in China

Written by Yan kejia
Translated by Chen shujie

CHINA   INTERCONTINENTAL   PRESS

TABLE OF CONTENTS

The Catholic Three
Church after the Founding of PRC /102

Chapter four
The Catholic Church in China After the Reform /123

PREFACE

Catholicism is foreign to China. There are many different opinions on when Catholicism was first introduced into China in the world of academia. According to Da Qin Jing Jiao Liu Xing Zhong Guo Bei (the Memorial of the Propagation in China of the Luminous Religion from Daqin), which was unearthed in 1626 in Xian, the majority of the scholars agreed that Christianity was first introduced into China was in Tang Dynasty in the 7th Century. But Jing Jiao, which was first introduced into China, was one denomination of Christianity, not the Catholic Church which this book talks about.

In 1293, it was still Yuan Dynasty in China, Pope officially sent an Italian missionary whose name was John of Montecorvino to China. This was the first attempt of the Catholic Church to send missionaries to China. Unfortunately, following the overturn of the Yuan Dynasty, the Catholic Church was almost disappeared. In the 16th and 17th centuries, the Catholic Church made great progress in China and adapted Chinese culture accordingly because of the efforts that the Jesuits, such as Matteo Ricci, made when they came to China. Moreover, these Jesuit missionaries helped to promote the cultural and scientific exchanges between East and West. Because of this, the Catholic Church in China developed quite well. When the Rite Controversy broke out and intensified as time went on, the Catholic Church was suppressed for one hundred years. When the Opium War started, the Catholic missionaries reentered into China to evangelize the Chinese. Though the Church developed under the protection of the unequal treaties between China and other countries, it was rather unsteady and had numerous conflicts with the Chinese society. This affected the Church's localization terribly.

In 1949, the New China was founded which indicated that the Chinese Catholic Church entered into a new phase. The Catholics started an Anti-Imperialists and Pro-Patriotic Campaign and decided to self-manage the church affairs and to be more independent. This helped the Catholic Church to change its semi-colonial and semi-feudalist nature and eventually helped the

Church to continue its existence and development in the socialist China.

After half a century, especially, in the last 20 some years post the Chinese reform, since the Catholic Church insisted on the principle of the Three Self's (self administration, self-support, self propagation), it had its opportunity to continue its evangelization in China. The result was indeed tremendous. Up to the end of the last century, the Catholic population increased to 5,000,000; the reopened and newly built churches were more than 5600; there were 36 minor and major seminaries and 60 or so convents. The rights of religious freedom have been protected and the normal religious activities were resumed. The Chinese Catholic Church and the faithful have contributed greatly to the modernization of China and the world peace, as well as the mutual friendship among the peoples. The Chinese Catholic Church has earned its respect and honor from both China and abroad.

CHAPTER ONE
CATHOLIC CHURCH IN THE MING AND QING DYNASTIES

I. From Envoy to Missionary

Ever since the 13th century, Rome began to send envoys to the Yuan Emperor on numerous occasions. Few recorded materials on this missionary work have been found until the time of John of Monte Corvino (1247-1328), a Franciscan who was sent to China in 1291 by Pope Nicholas IV.

As the first Roman Catholic missionary to China, John came to China in 1294 from Quanzhou, traveling to Dadu to meet the Emperor and hand over a letter from the Pope. He obtained permission from the emperor to perform religious activities in Dadu, and was able to convert the Nestorian leader Kuo Li Ji Si of

◎ Remains of a typical Roman Catholic style church discovered in the old A Lun Si City located in Damao Prairie in Inner Mongolia. This was the oldest Catholic Church in Asia which had 700 years of history

Wang Gu Bu, and built a church in that place. In 1302, he built another church with a capacity of 200 not far from the palace. He translated the New Testament, the Psalms and various Latin rituals and prayers into the Mongolian dialect. John adopted about 40 children who were aged between 7 and 11 and taught them Greek and Latin. He taught them how to sing psalms and explained Bible stories to them. Eventually, he baptized all of them. In 1307, Rome named him as the archbishop of Han Ba Li (Beijing) and also sent another seven missionaries to China as his assistants. Unfortunately, four died in India en route, but the remaining three all became bishops of Quanzhou in due course.

A letter written by one of the three missionaries, whose name was Andrew, to a priest from his hometown who was teaching in the seminary, stated that he assisted John of Monte Corvino for five years in dealing with church affairs. The Yuan Emperor provided all the daily expenditures, also called alpha, while he was in Beijing. After he became the bishop of Quanzhou, he used the salaries provided by the Emperor to build a 'luxurious and comfortable church with all kinds of offices which were enough for 20 colleagues. There are also four other rooms that can be used for high-ranking priests [①] '. He died of illness in 1326 and the Diocese of Quanzhou was dissolved.

Archbishop John managed the Diocese of Beijing for over 30 years and claimed to have baptized more than 6,000 people. He died in 1328 at the age of 81. Upon hearing of his death five years later, Pope John XXII (1316-1334) sent Nicholas to Beijing to be the bishop, but he unfortunately died on the journey. Ten years later, in 1338, Pope Pius XII sent Giovani de Marignoli to China. Because of the unstable political situation of the Yuan Empire, however, he quickly returned to Rome. After the founding of Ming Dynasty, the Catholic Church in central China passed from the scene simply because most of the Catholics were Mongols.

2. Jesuits at the end of the Ming dynasty and their policies

From 1368 to 1644, the Catholic Church in China was somewhat moribund. This phenomenon lasted until the end of the Ming Dynasty. At the same time, Europe was going through many dramatic social changes: Feudalism was dissolved, and new countries were created based on races; the capitalistic system was developing in some European cities and modern technologies were assuming greater importance. Meanwhile, there were also changes occurring within the Catholic Church leading to religious reformation and the eventual emergence of the Protestant Church. Facing the rapid social progress and the influence of the religious reformation, the Catholic Church began to undergo internal changes by reorganizing the religious orders both old and new. They sent many missionaries abroad to proselytize in order to counteract the Reformation influence. Borrowing its own saying, the church was 'trying to gain what they had lost in Europe'. Under such circumstances, the Society of Jesus founded by

◎ Francis Xavior's Coffin in Guo A Ben Ji Tu Church, India

Ignatius of Loyola (1491-1556) came onto the scene in China and eventually exercised great influence.

Meanwhile, Spain and Portugal were trying to expand their colonies abroad. The Roman Curia also had the intention of promoting the Catholic faith abroad. Pope Alexander VI (1492-1503), in his Encyclical , *Inter Caetera* decided to give Africa and the East to the Portuguese as missionary territory. Portugal had the right to send out missionaries, build churches and seminaries, all at its own expense in this vast territory. The King of Portugal had the right to name bishops as well. This right is called

Patronatus Missionum in Latin.

Francis Xavier (1506-1552) was the first Jesuit who tried to enter China to preach the Gospel. Since it was forbidden for a non-Chinese to go inland, he arrived at Shangchuan Island in Taishan County in Guangdong Province in August of 1552, but died there on December 3rd in the same year. Although Francis never actually stepped penetrated inland, his enthusiasm for the China missionary work touched the hearts of a great number of Catholics both in China and abroad. They honored him with the title of Yuandong Kaijiao Zhi Yuan Xun, meaning Missionary Pioneer of the Far East.

Portugal made Macao a permanent transit location for them to penetrate China in 1554. Merchants flooded into Macao, and the church followed. Eventually, Macao became a center of Catholic missionary work in the Far East. Melchior Barreto arrived in Macao in 1555 and built a regular house as the first Catholic church [1]. Later, the Augustinians, Dominicans and Franciscans, Jesuits and others found their respective places in Macao, but the Jesuits were the most dominant and influential. The Jesuits established St. Paul's Seminary, the first Catholic university in China, offering courses in philosophy, theology and Latin. It had a library, observatory and medical supplies' depot.

[1] Fei Cheng Kang, Macao Si Bainian, Shanghai People's Press, 1987. p53

◎ Da San Ba Wall is a famous historical site. It was the front wall of Da San Ba Church which was also called Saint Paul's Church. The construction was started in 1602 and was completed in 1637. It was the biggest Catholic church in the Far East. A fire broke out in 1835 and destroyed the whole church but the front wall which was built with stones

The Diocese of Macao was officially created on January 23rd, 1576 to administer China, Amman, Japan and nearby islands. D. Leonard De Sa was appointed the first bishop of Macao in 1578. There were eight Catholics churches in Macao. St. Paul's Cathedral, which was constructed in 1602, was the most magnificent church in the Far East. Its construction took 35 years to complete. Macao's unique geographical location made it the ideal transit point for Catholic missionaries to enter China. Those missionaries wanting to work in China had first to go to the semi-nary in Macao to learn the language and Chinese culture before they could move on. At the end, most of those missionaries who were expelled from China went to Macao after the founding of the New China. Some of them stayed there to wait for fresh opportunities to occur, but others returned to Europe. Many of them who died are certainly buried in Macao.

Initially, the missionaries in Macao thought Western culture was superior to Chinese culture, and the small number of Chinese Catholics in Macao were forced to learn the Portuguese language and to take Portuguese names in order to isolate them from Chinese culture. The Jesuit priest Allessandro Valignani, Inspector of the Far East, realized the importance of changing the missionary mentality of despising things Chinese. He insisted that China was a civilized country with a long and glorious history, therefore, the missionaries wanting to work in China should mas-

◎ Matteo Ricci

ter the Chinese language in order to converse with both educated and non-educated Chinese in order to inspire them to accept Christianity. In 1582, he sent Michael Ruggieri (1543-1607), Matteo Ricci and others to Macao to study Chinese language and culture. When Valignani first came to China in 1580 with the merchants, his complaisant behavior and fluent Chinese earned respect from local officials. He was given permission to stay in the residence used by Thailand's consul.

The one who would actually raise the Jesuits' missionary spirit to a higher level was the Italian Matteo Ricci. Because of his hard work, the Catholic Church was able to succeed in China. Ricci and Valignani

◎ The Catholic church in Guxi villiage, Chaoyang county, Guangdong Province was combination of two churches: one old and one new. The older church was build in 1882 and the new one was added onto the old one in 1910

went to Zhaoqing together in 1583 and built a European style church outside the West gate alongside the Chongning Pagoda. The local official Wang Pan presented the church with a tablet inscribed Xian Huan Ci. Ricci hung a map of the world he had brought from Europe on the hall wall. He named the map as *Shan Hai Yu Di Quan Tu* (map of the world) He displayed all kinds of astronomical instruments, which attracted inspection by many elite people. Ricci and others used the opportunity to explain the Catholic catechism and five them books on the subject.

In order to spread the Gospel in China, Ricci tried to live his life in a Chinese way. When he first came to China, he shaved his head and wore Buddhist monk's robes and called himself a 'monk from the West'. Later, he changed to the Confucian style because he discovered that Confucianism was more dominant. Moreover, he knew exactly the way to make the Catholic Church known in China. He had to know the social elite and, through them, the dominant and most respected group in the country, in order to establish Christianity in China. Ricci, therefore, decided to study Confucian classics with the help of Qu Taisu, a Chinese scholar. Ricci was familiar with Si Shu Wu Jing and called himself a Confucian from the West. China's elites were amazed when they talked with Ricci because he quoted from the Chinese classics often. He traveled from Nanjing to Nanchang to preach and to make friends with the government officials, prominent people and elite scholars. He studied Chinese politics in order to seek an opportunity to go to Beijing. On May 18th, 1600, he got permission to go Beijing with help from Qu Taisu. When he arrived in the capital, he presented his credentials to the emperor, describing himself as a Western minister who admired Chinese culture and history. He did not mention his own missionary purpose in China. He stayed in Beijing thereafter.

Allessandro Valignani was happy with what Ricci had done, and decided to send more Jesuits to China in 1603. Matteo Ricci, Diego De Pantoja, and Gaspard Ferreira were in Beijing; Joao de Rocha, Pierre Ribeiro, Alphonsus Vagnoni and Felicien de Silva were in Nanjing; Emmanuel Diaz Sr. was in Nanchang; Nicholas Longobardi and Bartholomew Tedeschi were in Shaozhou. Those Jesuits were administering Church affairs in different capacities under Ricci's leadership. In 1605, Ricci bought Beijing Huiyuan, which became the church of Nantang later, in the Xuanwumen area in order to be able to meet the elite and scholars. By then, about 200 had been baptized and many of these newly baptized were high-ranking government officials.

In May 1610, Matteo Ricci died of illness at age of 59.

The success of the Jesuit mission in China was because they took the right way to adapt to Chinese culture and Chinese customs, showing respect as they preached the Gospel. They did not think "that Confucianism conflicted with Catholicism". [1] They studied the Chinese language and culture in order to introduce Western culture and science to China, as well as Catholicism. Emperor Kangxi called this way of evangelization the Rules of Matteo Ricci. Modern researchers, both in China and abroad, who are interested in the history of the Catholic Church have defined that way of evangelization as adaptable rule. [2]

The missionary activities of Ricci in China were a successful mingling of the two cultures. This can be described as the following: first of all, he introduced Western science and a new way of thinking to China. His writings and translations covered many fields: astronomy, calendar, geography, mathematics, geometry, mechanics, logic, music, ethics and methods of memorization. He earned fame in China *Zhu Shu Duo Ge Yan, Jie Jiao Jie Ming Shi*, which means he wrote books and many of his sayings became proverbs; all his friends were famous elite. Secondly, he tried to adapt Confucianism to Catholicism. In his book *The True Meaning of* the *Lord of Heaven*, the terms

[1] From Sun Shang Yan, Ji Du Jiao yu Ming Mo Ru Xue, Dongfang Press, 1994. p.51
[2] Zhang Kai, Pang Di Wo yu Zhong Guo : Ye Su Hui Shiying Ce Lue Yan Jiu, Beijing Library Press, 1997. p81

he explained Shangdi and Tian, which were used in Chinese classics *Zhou Song* as Tianzhu (God). He explained that the term Tianzhu was the one that the Chinese classics called Shangdi. [1] He used many ethical codes that the Chinese elite could accept to prove the existence of God: "The first of these arguments has to do with humankind's untutored

◎ Xu Guangqi and Matteo Ricci

ability, which is innate ability"[2] 'Now, men of all nations under heaven possess, each of them, a natural capacity by which, without any communication between them, all venerate One which is regarded as worthy of supreme honor.' In order not to conflict with Chinese thinking habits and traditional thoughts, Ricci did not mention much about the doctrines of the Trinity, the Crucifixion and the Resurrection of Jesus. As a result, some people later criticized him for introducing a senseless religion to the

①   Zhu Wei Zhen,(editor) Li Ma Dou Zhong Wen Zhu Yiji, from Tian Zhu Shi Yi,
     Fu Dan University Press,2001. p21
②   Ibid. p.9

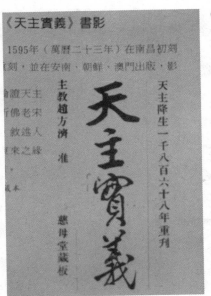

《天主寶義》書影

1595年（萬曆二十三年）在南昌初刻

刻，並在安南·朝鮮·澳門出版，影

會證天主

主教道方濟

天主降生一千八百六十八年重刊

行佛老宋

准

敘述人

宋之降

慈母堂藏板

本

◎ Cover of the book True meaning of the Lord of Heaven

Chinese. Yet, the fact was that many scholars accepted his teachings. Xu Guanqi, a well-known scholar, was baptized into the Church after he read Ricci's book *The True Meaning of the Lord of Heaven*. Thirdly, Ricci introduced Chinese humanitarian thought, history and culture, as well as the life of Catholic Missionaries in China to Europe through his letters and reports. One of his works Ye Su Huishi Li Ma Dou Shenfu de Ji Du Jiao Yuan Zhen Zhong Guo Shi (Jesuit Priest Matteo Ricci on the History of Christianity in China), written in Latin, became a best seller. It was translated into French, German, Italian and other languages. In fact, chapters of that book were letters and reports the missionaries sent home. This deepened European academia's understanding of China and greatly influenced Europe in the early period of Enlightenment. A country that was in good order, tremendous wealthy and with a rich culture, which was managed in a way not based on God's Revelation, surprised many great European thinkers, such as Germany's Leibnitz. In their minds, China became an ideal country and they used this to criticize their own societies and thoughts.

3. Three Pillars of the Church at the End of Ming Dynasty

Because of the hard work of Jesuits such as Matteo Ricci, the Catholic Church finally established roots in China. By the time of his death, there were already four churches located in four different places: Beijing, Nanjing, Nanchang and Shaozhou. There were 13 European priests, seven Chinese seminarians with a congregation of about 2,000. Before he died, Ricci told Didago de Pantoia SJ, Sabbatino de Ursis SJ, as well as two Chinese seminarians, You Wenhui and Zhong Mingren: 'I have opened a grand door for you. If you go in through this door, you will do great works.' [1]

The appreciation that the early Jesuits showed towards Chinese culture earned the respect of Chinese officials and intellectuals. In return, those officials made it much easier for the missionaries to work in China. Some of them were even attracted by the teachings of the Catholic Church and were eventually baptized, the most well known being the scholars Xu Guangqi, Li

[1] Jiang Wenhan, Ming Qing Jian Zai Hua de Tian Zhu Jiao Ye Su Hui Shi, Zhi Shi Press, 1989. p19

Zhicao and Yang Tingjun. Because of their contributions to the Catholic missionary work in China, they were called the 'Three Pillars of the Catholic Church in the Ming Dynasty'.

Xu Guangqi (1562-1633) was born in Xu Jiahui, Shanghai. He saw the *Shan Hai yu Di Quan Tu* (The map of the world) when he was young and be-gan to show his admiration for Father Matteo Ricci. In the spring of 1600, Xu Guangqi was delighted to meet Ricci for the first time in Nanjing. The latter started to teach him the Catholic Catechism. In 1603, Xu spent eight days in Nanjing to study Ricci's book *The True Meaning of the*

◎ Xu Guangqi

Lord of Heaven (Tianzhu Shi Yi) and was baptized by Father Joao de Rocha SJ. His Christian name was taken after the Apostle Paul. In 1604, Xu earned the title Jinshi after he passed the na-tional exam for scholars and entered Hanlin Academy. Eventu-ally, he became an official in charge of imperial ceremonies and a scholar in the Wen Yuange in the imperial court.

Xu Guangqi was a scholar who could utilize his knowledge well. He was the foremost scholar to learn and to introduce Western science to China. In the fall of 1605, Matteo Ricci and Xu Guangqi began to translate Euclid's Elements (Ji He Yuan Ben) into Chinese. It was a milestone of the cultural exchanges between the West and China. Over a period of one year, Xu came to Ricci's house every afternoon around three or four o'clock to work with him. As Ricci spoke, Xu recorded all his words. Eventually, the first six books of the Elements were pub-

◎ a page picture of Euclid's Elements

lished. Because of the extraordinary quality of this translation, the terms they used for Geometry: Dian (point), Xian (line), Zhixian (straight line), Pingmian (Plane), Quxian (Curved line), are still in use today. The most important aspect of this book is that it introduced the strict Western scholastic logic method into China and became the foundation of its development. Chinese intellectuals highly appreciated the book. After Xu's death, Emperor Wan Li donated a piece of land for his burial. This caused some resentment among some officials, eliciting a response from Ye Xianggao, an official from the Imperial ceremonial court, as follows: 'You have not seen any foreigner who was granted a piece of land for burial in the past. Have you seen anyone whose knowledge surpassed Matteo Ricci? Simply, the book Elements (Ji He Yuan Ben) is the first and the greatest book in Chinese history. Its contribution is immeasurable. Merely because of this, the Emperor should grant him a piece of land for burial.' [1]

At the end of the Ming Dynasty, those intellectuals, who accepted the Catholic teachings, did so mainly because they found similarities between the two cultures. Xu Guangqi, in his book *Bian Xue Zhang Shu* (Chapters on distinquished learning), wrote about the Catholic Church as follows: 'The Church teaches people to be kind, which leads to knowledge of the Truth; to avoid evil which leads to purity. The Church teaches God's creation and salvation history, as well as the meaning of rewarding the good and punishing the evil. Anyone who understands the true teachings of the Church will be moved by it.' The Catholic Church can 'help the Emperor to safeguard the Kingdom, to control the development of Confucian culture and to correct the Buddhist methods'. Simply, it is 'Bu Ru Yi Fo' (adding what

[1] Ai Ru Lue, Da Xi Li Xian Shen Xing Ji, from Jiang Wen Han, Ming Qing Jian Zai Hua de Tian Zhu Jiao Ye Su Hui Shi, Zhi Shi Press, 1989, p28

Confucian culture lacks, correcting what is wrong in Buddhism).

Li Zhicao and Yang Tingjun, who were Xu Guangqi's contemporaries, were also well-known Catholics. Li Zhicao (1565-1630), a native of Renhe (Hangzhou), in Zhejiang Province, also had another Chinese name, Zhenzhi. He became Juren in 1594 and Jinshi in 1598. In a variety of capacities, he took many offices in the imperial court over the years: Gongbu Shusi Liangzhong, Nanjing Taipuci Shaoqing, Hedao Gongbu Langzhong, Guangdong Buzhenshi, Guangluci Shaoqing, etc. In 1611, he was finally baptized into the Church and took the Christian name of Leo. Very early on, Li began to learn the natural sciences from Ricci, such as astronomy, geography and mathematics. He worked with Ricci to translate books on these subjects into Chinese, such as Hun Gai Tong Xian Tu Shuo, Tong Wen Suan Zhi and Huan Rong Jiao Yi. In 1628, when he was well advanced in age, he edited and published the first series of Catholic Books Tian Xue Chu Han. These collected 20 kinds of writings and translations of both science and religion from missionaries and lay people. The books were divided into two parts: Li ' 理 ' (religion) and Qi ' 器 '. They were well accepted by all.

Li Zhicao's understanding of Catholicism was based on his

understanding of Confucianism. He made a famous statement: 'Dong Hai Xi Hai, Xin Tong Li Tong'[①] which means the heart of the matter is the same between East and West. He claimed the knowledge that the Jesuits had was called 'Knowledge of Heaven' which is compatible with Confucian culture: Knowing Tian (Heaven), serving Tian, do not oppose the principles of Liu Jing. 'This is the root of life. Its meaning and principle prevailed. This has not been discussed previously.'[②] Li Zhicao's understanding and interpretation of the part 'microscopic and root of life', which is also in the Catholic Catechism, came from the Confucian self-cultivation and serving one's neighbors' theory. In his book *Tianzhu Shiyi Chong Ke Xu*, he wrote: 'Once you know the truth, you should put it into practice. Serving Tian and serving neighbors are the same, however, Tian is the source of all matters. The universe has one Lord who is the Lord of all. This is self-evident and is in line with our classical teachings. The core of Ricci's knowledge is serving Tian, therefore, the concept of Tian is extremely clear in his teachings.'[③]

Yang Tingjun (1557-1627), was a native of Renhe. In 1592, he became Jinshi, and in 1598, he became Jian Cha Yushi. Later, he fell out of favor and returned home. While staying at home teaching, he developed a strong interest in Buddhism. After dis-

① Ibid. p110
② Li Zhi Cao, Ke Tian Xue Chu Han Ti Ci, from Xu Zong Ze, Ming Qing Jian Ye Su Hui Shi Yi Zhu Ti Yao, Zhong Hua Shu Ju, 1989, p286
③ Zhu Wei Zhen (editor), p.99

cussing Catholicism with Lazaro Cattaneo SJ and Nicholas Trigault SJ, Yang was baptized and took the name of Michael. After his conversion from Buddhism to Catholicism, he became more enthusiastic in religion, which caused criticism from Buddhists. In refuting this criticism, he wrote many apologetic and pro-missionary articles that were widely spread, such as Dai Yi Pian and Dai Yi Xu Pian. He thought that the Catholic dogma and Confucian thought were compatible. However, he thought the true Confucian thought had already been lost. The Western thought which Ricci brought to China, that 'Heaven is the source of all, and there is only one Lord of Heaven who is the most high [is a] teaching true and clear, and is the same as the teaching of our Classics.' [①]

Many Chinese intellectuals were baptized into the Catholic Church. Wang Zheng (1571-1644), a native of Jingyang, Shaanxi, was one such. He began to study Western science from the missionaries and worked with Johan Terrentius SJ (1576-1630) to translate *Yuan Xi Qiqi Tu Shuo* (Instructions of western Instruments)into Chinese. This was the first book on Mechanics and Machinery available in China. Han Lin, a native of Jiangzhou, Shaanxi, became Juren in 1621. He studied military strategy from Xu Guangqi and, because of Xu's influence, became a Catholic.

① Ibid. p206

Li Yingshi, Jin Shen, Chen Yujie, Han Yun, Han Xian, Zhang Geng, Qu Shikui, Qu Shigu, Qu Shisi, Li Tianjing, Li Zubai, Zhang Xingyao, Chu Jinan, Ding Yuntai, etc. were other well-known Chinese Catholics.

Those Chinese intellectuals contributed greatly to the Catholic mission in China. First of all, they translated Western scientific works into Chinese. They were pioneers of the intellectuals who had a world vision. Secondly, they provided opportunities for the Catholic Church to preach the Gospel in China. Because of their engagement, the Catholic Church built many churches in various places. For example, when his father died in 1607, Xu Guangqi went home according to the custom of the day to stay for three years. When he passed by Nanjing, he invited Lazaro Catteneo SJ. to go to Shanghai. He built a church in his home and more than 50 people from his family were baptized, including children, relatives and servants. Later on, more than 150 people came into the Church. This was the first group of Catholics in Shanghai. More and more people were baptized as time went on. By the mid-17th century, the Catholic population reached 3,000. In 1661, the administrator of the local Church, Father Pan Guoguang, informed the Jesuit Superior General that the increase of the Catholic population was 200 annually, which made Shanghai the fastest growing Catholic community in the Jiangnan region. The reason why the Catholic Church could grow in China at the end of Ming Dynasty was obvious: not only did the missionaries use a strategy acceptable to both Chinese society and its culture, but also Chinese Catholic intellectuals made great efforts and show great willingness to work for the Church.

During the first half of the 17th century, the Chinese Catholics were mainly located in Shanghai and Jiangnan regions. The population increased from 13,000 in 1627 to 40,000 ten years later. By then, the Catholics were spread through many provinces: Jiangxi, Zhejiang, Jiangnan, Shandong, Shaanxi, Shanxi and Zhili. By the year 1661, Catholics were to be found in all 15 provinces except for Yunnan and Guizhou.

4. Well-Accepted Missionaries by the Qing Emperor

Adam Schall

Since the time of Matteo Ricci, many Jesuits stayed in Beijing. They were all well educated and specialized in certain areas of Western science, knowledge that could be utilized and employed by the Emperor. Some of them earned imperial trust and were made officials of the Imperial Court. After the Qing Dynasty was established, the Jesuits continued to be highly regarded by the Emperors. The well-known ones among them were Adam Schall SJ (1591-1666) and Ferdinandus Verbiest SJ (1623-1688).

The tradition to utilize the missionaries' scientific knowledge can trace back to Xu Guangqi. In 1629, Emperor Chongzhen decided to create a department to revise the old calendar. Xu Guangqi was the head of the department and Li Zhicao was his assistant. The greatest work that this department had done was to finish the Chongzhen Calendar of 137 volumes. These volumes that explained systematically Western astrological theories were presented five times to the Emperor between 1631-

1634. Xu Guangqi invited many missionaries who had acquired certain expertise in science to work for him, such as Adam Schall, Johan Terrentius and Giacomo Rho, especially Terrentius, a German, who was a scientist in the Papal Science Institute. In Europe, he was famous for his rich knowledge in medicine, philosophy and mathematics. When he came to China, he brought with him the works of Nicolai Copernicus' Heliocentric System, Johannes Kepler's Outline of Copernicus' Astronomy, as well as the work of Galileo and others. He went to work with Xu in 1629. Within six months, he wrote Ce Tian Yue Shou in two volumes; Da Ce in two volumes and Li Shu Zong Mulu. He edited many other scientific works and directed the building of two instruments called Qi Zhen Xiang Xian. Because of a heavy workload, he died two years later at age of 55. Xu Guangqi highly credited the missionaries in his report to the Emperor: 'They wrote and translated books and made all kinds of tabulations, and they built scientific instruments. They did not have time to eat and no time to sleep. They were like the stars moving all the time. They had also to teach other people in the department. The heavy load almost made them become bald and their words nearly burned their lips. They deserve to be acknowledged.' [①]

In the second year of Emperor Shun Zhi, the government

① Xu Guang Qi, Xu Guang Qi Ji vol. 2, Zhong Hua Shu Ju, 1962, p427 discovered that the Solar Eclipse did not occur according to the existing calendar. As a result, Adam Schall was named as the imperial Jianzheng to revise the calendar. In the following year, the newly edited Xi Yang Xing Fa Li Shu was submitted to the Emperor. It had 103 volumes and was based on Chongzhen Li Shu. The Emperor was delighted in Schall and even promoted him three times in one day. He was promoted from 'Tong Yi Da Fu' to 'Tai Pu Ci Qing' to 'Tai Chang Ci Qing'. Simply put, Schall's position jumped from 'Wu Pin' to Yi Pin'. The Emperor himself even called Schall as 'Mafa', meaning Master in Manchurian.

The Emperor often went to Schall's residence to talk about astronomy and imperial politics. Meanwhile, Schall could come to visit the Emperor without the usual complicated rituals of kneeling and kowtow required for all other officials.

◎ Snow scene of Beijing Xuan Wu Men Catholic church, which is also called Nantang

In 1650, Adam Schall built a new European style church at the place where Ricci had built the first one, which is known as

Nan Tang. In 1652, Emperor Shun Zhi granted a framed 'Qing Chong Tian Dao' (to adore the Heavenly Principle) to hang above the altar. This brought great honor to the Catholic Church. A year later, he honored Schall with the title of 'Tong Xuan Jiao Shi' for his tremendous work on revising the calendar. In 1654, the Emperor gave a piece of land outside of

© Adam Schall works in his office

Fu Cheng Men as Ricci's graveyard. In 1657, the Emperor in his Yu Zhi Tian Zhu Tang Bei Ji praised Schall with the words 'Ren Shi You Nian, Yi Qing Jue Zhi', which means he devoted himself to his work for numerous years. The Emperor understood Schall's Catholic Faith: 'After spending many years in China, Adam Schall could still be faithful to his Faith and worshiping his God,......' The Emperor thought that was the reason why Schall could faithfully serve the Emperor and yet fulfill his own duties.

From Matteo Ricci to Adam Schall, the Jesuit missionaries kept a good relationship with the Imperial court. This was also the reason why the Catholic Church could grow steadily both at the end of the Ming Dynasty and in the early years of the Qing Dynasty. The country's rulers needed the scientific knowledge of the missionaries for the good of China, and missionaries needed a good relationship with, and the support of the rulers so that the Church could remain on good terms with Chinese society. Because of this, the Catholic Church grew quickly in China during the second part of the 17th century. From 1651 to 1664, the Catholic population in China reached 100,000, scattered in many provinces, such as Zhili, Shandong, Shanxi, Shaanxi, Henan, Sichuan, Huguang, Jiangxi, Fujian, Zhejiang, Jiangnan, etc..

Ferdinandus Verbiest

Ferdinandus Verbiest (1623-1688), a native of Belgium, graduated from Leuven Catholic University. He arrived in China in 1659 and began his ministry in Shaanxi Province. At the recommendation of Schall, he went to Beijing to help work on the Calendar-revision project. Verbiest was once arrested and questioned. Later, he took Yang Guanxian's position and was in charge of the imperial ceremonial work. He wrote to Emperor Kang Xi to rectify the condemnation the previous Emperor imposed on Adam Schall and others. He worked very hard to get all the missionaries in Guangzhou released from prison. His tremendous impetus on the revitalization of the Church's missionary affairs in China was beyond description.

After he was named the Jesuit Superior in the China missions in 1676, he wrote an article, To all European Jesuits, calling on them to support the work in China. Out of business interests and perceived benefits of colonization, King Louis XIV sent some scholars who were Jesuits from the France Science & Technology Institute to China, including Johannes de Fonteney (1643-1710), Jeannes Franciscus Gerbillon (1654-1707) and Joachim Bouvet (1656-1730), as well as two others. Carrying 30 boxes of astronomy instruments, they arrived in Ningbo in March, 1685 and traveled on to Beijing in February 1688. Jeannes Franciscus Gerbillon and Joachim Bouvet stayed in Beijing, while the others awaited assignment. [1] They were the first group of French Jesuit missionaries in China.

Verbiest's contribution in sciences is obvious to all. He pointed out Yang Guangxian's mistakes and corrected them in the revision of the Western Calendar. He got rid of the so-called

① Huang Bo Lu, Zheng Jiao Feng Bao, p88

saying, 'Zi Qi' and made the revised Chinese calendar more scientific. When he was in charge
of the revision project, he tried
to advise the government to improve the official economic and
political remuneration, especially for the Chinese. On the
other hand, he took many missionaries who were specialists
into his office, such as Navarrete

© Ferdinandus Verbiest

(1624-1684), Nicolas Fiva (1645-1708) and Anthony (1644-
1709). There were two people who were in charge of the office:
one Manchurian, one Westerner, as well as numerous missionaries who worked there. The situation of having foreign missionaries work in that office lasted until Emperor Dao Guang (1817).

In 1669, Verbiest was ordered to fix the instruments in the
Observatory. Besides the old Jia Yi, Hun Yi, Xing Qiu, he also
made Tian Qiuyi, Huang Dao Theodolite, Ji Xian Yi, Xiang Xian
Yi, Di Ping Jing Yi and Di Ping Wei Yi. All these instruments
required extremely careful designs. Every line on the instruments
was precise, and they were all very artistic. All the instruments

for the Observatory were ready in 1674 as planned. Verbiest wrote down a 14-volume detailed instruction, including the process of making them, their use and the measured results. Later, he wrote Yi Xiang Tu in two volumes. Verbiest gave them to all the officials. Emperor Kang Xi said in praise, 'calendar and astronomy are extremely important to the county. I have heard all the instruments were made and were extremely accurate. Verbiest put all his heart into this and therefore he needs to be rewarded.' [1]

In 1688, Verbiest fell from horseback while riding and died. Emperor Kang Xi honored him with the title 'Qing Min', and provided 750 pieces of silver to build a tomb with a tombstone. He sent an official to the tomb to offer his condolences and honored him on another tombstone declaring: 'From your hands, we have stored sufficient necessary military staff.' The 'sufficient necessary military staff' were the 132 powder guns. They were used when Kang Xi defeated 'San Fang Zhi Luan'. When the Qing Government tried to get back Ya Ke Sa, the powder guns scared the Russians away.

[1] Ibid. p72

5. *Kang Xi's 'Toleration Edict'*

After the death of Verbiest, other missionaries continued their work at the imperial court. In 1689, when China and Russia negotiated their disputes over their common border, the Jesuit priests Jeannes Franciscus Gerbillon and Grimaldi were the Latin translators on behalf of China. Behind the scenes, the Russians tried to persuade the priests to speak on their behalf and told them not to allow China to build houses in Ya Ke Sa. This the Jesuits refused to do. On September 7, 1689, the Sino-Russian Treaty of Nerchinsk was signed by the two parties on an equal basis. The missionaries were crucial during the negotiating process. Emperor Kang Xi was pleased with the them and said: 'The Treaty could be signed was because of your wisdom and hard work. You have done a great job.'[1] Later, all these French Jesuits, such as Thomas Pereira, Franciscus Gerbillon and Joachim Bouvet, were invited to go to the Emperor's residence to teach him about various Western subjects, namely Liang Fa, Ce San, Tian Wen and Ge Zhi. This work lasted many years.

① Xu Ri Sheng Diary, from Jiang Wen Han, Ming Qing Jian Zai Hua de Tian Zhu Jiao Ye Su Hui Shi, Zhi Shi Press, 1989, p77

In 1693, Kang Xi contracted malaria and Gerbillon prescribed him some medicine, which soon achieved a cure. Because of this, the Emperor granted a piece of land to erect a Catholic church, which was Beitang in Beijing. Emperor Kangxi came to visit this church twice and gave a framed banner 'Wan You Zhen Yuan' and two couplets which read, 'Wu Shi Wu Zhong, Xian Zuo Xing Sheng Zhen Zhu Zai; Xuan Ren Xuan Yi,Yu Zhao Zheng Ji Da Quan Heng'. He also wrote two words: 'Jing Tian' which hung inside the church.

◎ Catholic Missionary dressed in Chinese Official's Uniform (Sanpin) in the early twentieth century

The attitude of Qing government was to allow the missionaries to be free to preach. It is uncertain whether the missionaries could preach in the countryside because there is no record found in this regard. There were missionaries in the hinterland, most of them were there for such stated purposes as 'staying', 'paying tribute to their dead parents' or 'retreating from the world', and not carrying out church work.

Things eventually changed dramatically, but at first the signs were good. In the 31st year of the reign of Kang Xi (1692), he issued two orders sequentially and the Imperial ceremonial department carried out his order, '...the Westerners did not do anything to break the law. It is not appropriate if we forbid them from preaching. Keep the Catholic churches there without being destroyed. Do not prevent those who go to temples to pray or to offer incense. After the order is issued, all the provinces should observe it. This was greatly appreciated by the missionaries. They hailed this edict as 'long-awaited Christian Toleration Edict.' ①
This indicated that the missionaries could freely preach the Catholic doctrine among the peoples who could be baptized into the church. Thus, the Catholic Church had entered into another important phase.

Besides the presence of the Jesuits in China, other religious orders also entered. In the years of 1626 and 1629, the Dominicans built churches in Jilong and Danshui, Taiwan. 1630, Gao Qi, a Dominican, went on mission to Dingtou in Fujian Province. In 1633, Li Yufan also came to Fujian. In 1650, the Franciscan priest Li Andang went to Jinan, Shandong Province

① J. Luo Ke Man, Ye Su Hui Shi You Ji Xuan (1698, 1/11) vol. 2 London, 1743, p107

and built a church there. The number of baptisms reached 1,500 soon. Although those Franciscans and Dominicans received a cold reception from the Catholics who had been baptized by the Jesuits, they finally stabilized their missions. In 1665, the Dominicans had 11 residences, 20 churches with about 10,000 believers in Zhenjiang, Fujian and Guangdong provinces.

In order to take back the powers over the missionaries from Spain and Portugal, Rome decided to use the Apostolic Vicariate system. The Apostolic delegate had the same power as the local bishop, but he acted on the Pope's behalf and came under the leadership of the Congress of the Propagation of the Faith. In the turmoil of the power struggle, the French church decided to take Rome's side out of its own interests. In 1663, the French church formed a missionary group (Foreign Missions), its founder being Francois Pallu who came to Zhangshou, Fujian Province in 1684. Calling himself the 'Premier of China Church Affairs'①, he sent a pastoral letter to all the missionaries in China asking them to come before him to pledge their obedience to Rome in order to keep things in order. However, Pallu died that year and so the thing never went too far.

Rome continued its Apostolic delegate system. In 1693, it decided to divide China into 12 regions with three distinct dio-

① Xu Zong Ze, Zhog Guo Tian Zhu Jiao Shi Gai Lun (microfilm), Shanghai Bookstore, 1990, p229

ceses: Nanjing, Beijing and Macao. Guangdong and Guangxi belonged to Macao diocese; Jiangnan, Henan belonged to the Nanjing Diocese; Zhili, Shandong and Liaodong belonged to Beijing. The rest were Apostolic Vicariates: namely, Yunnan, Sichuan, Zhejiang, Jiangxi, Huguang, Shanxi, Shaanxi and Guizhou. The reason why Rome did this was, it was said, because Emperor Kangxi had issued the Toleration Edict in the previous year, and the Vatican thought it was easier for the local churches to be managed if there were more dioceses added on to the list. [①]

While this was going on, the enculturation process was also taken place. China had its first Catholic bishop Luo Wencao (1616-1691), a native of Fu'an, Fujian Province. He was baptized in 1633 and went to Nanjing and Beijing on missions with Li Andang. He joined the Dominicans in 1650 and was ordained to the priesthood in 1654 in Manila. During the years of Li Yu, he began to take on the responsibilities of church affairs in China and baptized over 2,000 converts. In 1674, Pope Clement X named Luo Wencao as the bishop of Basilica and the Apostolic delegate of Nanjing diocese. Because he stood on the Jesuit's side during the China Rite Controversy, the Dominican Superior General Jia Delang, who was in the Philippines, refused to have him consecrated. Later in 1685, Luo was ordained a bishop in Guangzhou by Bernardinus Della Chiesa (1642-1721), a native of Italy.

Luo and Chiesa sought permission from Rome to allow the Chinese seminarians to be ordained, but failed. In 1688, Luo ordained three Chinese young men to the priesthood. When the China Rite Controversy became more and more severe, Luo wrote to the Congress of the Propagation of the Faith, warning them to be careful in dealing with the matter. He asked the Vatican not to forbid the Chinese rite, because this could cause harm to the church. In 1690, Luo was named the bishop of Nanjing. Because of his tireless work, he became ill and died on February 27, 1691.

Among the three ordained Chinese priests, Wu Yushan (1632-1718) was the most famous. He was a native of Changshu, Jiangsu Province and a famous painter. He was baptized around the year 1675 and his baptismal name was Simon Xavier. After his ordination in 1688, he went to Shanghai to preach the Gospel for about 30 years. He was very pious and left many poems describing religions and the Christian missions. Dan Yuan Chang Nian Neng Jian Mu, Chao Wang Dong Nan Mu Xi Bei (I hope that I can do my ministry all year long, I go to the South-East in the morning and go to the North-West in the evening); Du Pu Du Pu Mou Chi Wu, Lai Chao Gu Bing Pu Xi Lu (Going across the Huang Pu River back and forth to do my ministry without delay; In the Future, when I get sick, I go to Pi Xi Road to visit doctors).[1] He died in Shanghai in 1718 and was buried in the Jesuit cemetery outside Our Lady's Parish Church. He wrote *Mo Jing Shi Chao, San Ba Ji* and *Mo Jing Ti Ba*. Each book had one volume, later, some author wrote a five-volume Mo Jing Ji. Wu also left a book that was a collection of his homilies. [2]

During the 17th and 18th Century, the Catholic Church in China enjoyed its most prosperous time. In 1701, there were 229 churches and 103 foreign missionaries with 300,000 registered Catholics. The enculturation movement gained some momentum, too. Luo Wencao was the first Catholic priest and bishop in history. Besides the Jesuits, other religious orders, such as the Dominicans, Franciscans and the Foreign Mission of Paris also sent their priests to China. Rome used the Apostolic Delegate system to control the Chinese work. Schall and Verbiest were the first group of Jesuits who developed Ricci's Xue Shu Chuan Jiao (Conversion of the Intellectuals). While these missionaries equipped with scientific knowledge worked for the emperors, they also created a fairly good environment for the Catholic faith

① Gu Yu Lu, Zhong Guo Tian Zhu Jiao de Guo Qu he Xian Zai, Shanghai Social Science Institute press, 1989, p37
② Ibid. p37

to grow. This led Emperor Kang Xi to issue his edict on toleration, so that this first group of missionaries obtained official permission to preach in China.

6. China Rite Controversy and the Century-Long Suppression of the Church

The development of the Catholic Church did not always go smoothly. From the viewpoint of the external environment of China, the precautions against it and the distrustfulness still existed; from within, a crisis was fermenting. There were disagreements in dealing with the Chinese Confucian culture, and this was obvious within the religious orders. The disagreements eventually caused the lengthy China Rite Controversy. Rome was rather indecisive in dealing with this matter when it first erupted; later, the Pope ended the controversy by ruling against the Jesuits and forbidding the practice of Chinese rites and ceremonies by paying tribute to the ancestors and to Confucius. This was the cause of the century-long suppression.

The China Rite Controversy mainly focused on two issues. One was ancient Chinese tradition of paying tribute to ancestors and to Confucius. Was this tradition a religious or secular one? The other one was the Chinese terms used for the Creator. The

◎ Our Lady of Lourdes Church in Hu Zhuang, Shandong Province, was one of the two pilgrimage places in China. The Church was rebuilt. The Church is built on the top of the mountain which is located on the west side of Hu Zhang. This church was build in 1895

disagreements started from within the Jesuits. Matteo Ricci's group denied the religiosity side of Chinese customs and said that Catholics could participate in such ceremonies. All the terms, Shangdi, Tian and Tianzhi, which were common among people, could be used in the Church. The other group, led by Nicholas Longobardi, thought such ceremonies should be regarded as idolatry by the Church and, therefore, should be condemned. In regard to the Chinese term for the Creator, only the latin Deus should be used. A meeting was called in Jiading in 1628 by the Jesuits from China and other countries, and they came to a consensus: paying tribute to ancestors and to Confucius was not idolatry, but was actually in accord with the fourth Commandment: namely, to honor one's parents.

In 1632, the Franciscan Li Andang and the Dominican Li Yufan went on missions to Fujian while all these disputes were again emerging among the faithful. They saw with their own eyes the ceremonies in which Chinese to paid tribute to their ancestors and the funeral rites. They were extremely surprised that the Jesuit priest Ai Rulue allowed the Chinese Catholics to do such things. Li Yufan went to Rome in 1643 and submitted a letter with 17 accusations regarding alleged Jesuit wrongdoings to the Pope. On September 12, 1645, the Vatican decided to forbid the use of the Chinese term Shangdi for God, neither could Chinese Catholics pay tribute to their ancestors and to Confucius This order greatly disturbed the Jesuits. They decided to send Wei Kuangguo (1614-1661) to Rome to defend their ministry in China. On March 23, 1656, Pope Alexander VII issued an order that Chinese rites and ceremonies were purely cultural and secular rather than religious. As long as these rituals were not against the fundamentals of the Catholic faith, believers could participate in them at their own discretion. They were allowed to be with other non-Christians during those celebrations as long as the Catholics proclaimed their faith.

During the period of Liyu, the missionaries in Guangzhou, who were under supervision, held a meeting on December 16th 1667, during which they discussed 42 questions related to the China missions and agreed to obey the Pope's 1656 order to the Jesuits. Only Anthony and one other declined to sign the agreement. Claudio Grimaldi, a Dominican who participated in the meeting and signed his name, left for Europe where he attacked the Chinese ceremonies as pagan activities, and also criticized the Jesuit stance.

In 1687, Carolus Maigrot, a priest from the Congregation of Paris Foreign Missions was named as Apostolic Delegate. On March 26, 1693, he sent a pastoral letter forbidding the China rites. The Jesuits who were in China, worried about the harm this would do to the China mission; sent Li Ming to France and Rome to defend them and to explain the reasons behind their stance. Since the religious orders and academia in Europe were fighting against the Jesuits, a theologian from University of Paris published a manifesto supporting Maigrot and against the China rites.

While the Jesuits tried gain understanding in Rome, they informed Emperor Kangxi about the disagreements on the China

rites. Agreeing with the Jesuits, the Emperor made his stand clear on November 19, 1700: 'Worshiping God, serving the Emperor and respecting parents and the elderly are the same universally. This is unchangeable.'

On November 20, 1704, Pope Clement XI agreed with the Congress of the Propagation of the Faith on the decision to forbid Chinese Catholics from following the China Rites and sent Bishop Duo Luo (1667-1710) as a special envoy to China to execute the order. This caused the direct confrontation between Rome and the Chinese government.

◎ Catholic church on the island of Weizhou, Guangxi, was built in 1869. The stones that the walls used were came from the seashore. Its tower is Gothic style. The Beauty of the church has made it become a tourist place

Emperor Kang Xi was concerned about the missionaries' activities in China and the issue of their administration, so he decided to intervene in their regulation. On December 31, 1706, he issued the following order: All missionaries in China must obtain permission from the government, and all those who refused to do so would be expelled from China. Up until 1715, there were 48 missionaries who obtained such permission, among which there were 29 Jesuits and nine Franciscans ① . Kang Xi treated these missionaries very well: ' You have obtained permission from the government, the local officials know where

① Gu Yu Lu, Zhong Guo Tian Zhu Jiao de Guo Qu he Xian Zai, Shanghai Social Science Institute press, 1989. p72

you are coming from and the local people will be pleased to join the church.'

When Bishop Duo Luo heard about the order from Kang Xi, he issued another pastoral letter announcing the Pope's decision on the China Rites. On March 15, 1715, Pope Clement XI published the encyclical *Ex Illa Dei*, in which he indicated his support for Bishop Duo Luo and asked all the missionaries in China to pledge their obedience to him in front of the Apostolic delegates or Bishops. Kang Xi was irritated upon hearing of Pope Clement XI's order and he decided to suppress the Church in China. In the order he issued, written in red ink, he declared: 'This order is only to those Western mean fellows. How could they understand China's great theory! Moreover, none of those Westerners know Chinese classics well and can express themselves well in Chinese. Most of them are laughable. From now on, all those Westerners should not be allowed to preach in China because they only can cause trouble.'

From then on, the Roman Curia insisted on their stand forbidding Catholics from participating in Chinese ceremonies. In 1742, Pope Benedict XIV (1740-1758) issued a letter entitled From God's Will to all the missionaries, asking them to comply with this decision; otherwise, they would be recalled to Europe

① Ibid. 71

and disciplined. This China Rite Controversy lasted right up to 1942, when Matteo Ricci's stand on the China Rites was finally reclaimed.

The China Rite Controversy was a major issue in the history of the Chinese Catholic Church. It lasted so long and covered many cultural areas that brought great harm to church affairs. Rome's decision to forbid Chinese Catholics to participate in Chinese ceremonies was the direct cause of Kang Xi deciding to suppress the Church. Later Emperors, such as Yong Zheng, Qian Long, Jia Qing and Dao Guang, followed the same course. Although Rome continued to send missionaries to China, they were all considered illegal in China and had to remain underground.

The Catholic Church, having been suppressed in 1717 by Emperor Kang Xi, was finally allowed to reopen in 1858 by Emperor Xian Feng under the barrels of foreign guns after a gap of 138 years. Catholics readily use the term 'century-long suppression' to describe the situation.

◎ Well-known Catholic church in Xu Jia Hui, Shanghai, was in Gothic style. During the 40s in the 17th century, western missionaries began to come to Shanghai, the Catholic Church and Protestant Churches were building churches there

CHAPTER TWO
CHINESE CATHOLIC CHURCH AFTER THE OPIUM WAR

1. Unequal Treaty and the opening of Catholic Activities

After the Opium War in 1842, China was defeated by Western military power and the Qing government was forced to sign a series of unequal treaties.

On August 29, 1842, China signed the Nanjing Treaty with the British government. This required China not only to give up Hong Kong and open five sea port cities to foreign trade, but also to protect the missionaries in China: 'The Catholic Church asks people to be good and holy. Therefore, all the missionaries who come to China from now on should be protected.' The one thing that is worth mentioning in the treaty is the Western view of separation of Church and State had been ignored. They interfered with an undermined China's own supreme authority. In October 1844, China signed another unequal treaty, the Huangpu Treaty, with France. The governor of Liang Guang, who participated in the negotiations, wrote to Emperor Dao Guang in December asking him to relax the rules on the Catholic Church but continue to forbid missionaries to go inland. In February 1846, Emperor Dao Guang issued an order to the whole country allowing Chinese to once again enter the Catholic Church and returning all the Catholic churches back to church control. The order made it also very clear that the missionaries should not go to inland to preach. This part of the order did not go too far before it was dismissed.

After China lost the second Opium War, many countries, including Russia, the United States, Britain and France, forced the Qing government to sign a further series of treaties. The Zhong Ying (Sino-UK) Tianjin Treaty stated: 'Jesus' holy Church is the Catholic Church, and it asks people to be holy and good. The Church asks people to treat others as they would like to be treated themselves. All those preach for this Church and those who learn about the Church should be protected. All Chinese officials have no rights over them'. Zhong Fa (Sino-French) Tianjin Treaty contained a similar statement: '...according to article eight, all those missionaries who have permission to go inland should be protected. In order to avoid punishment, local officials should have no rights to question them. All the places following the order to suppress the Church should stop doing so.' As a result, the Catholic mission expanded to all the provinces in China. In October 1860, China and France signed another treaty, the Zhong Fa Beijing Treaty, in which a Chinese official was induced by a priest from Paris Foreign Missions to add the following clause: 'Any French missionary can rent or buy land. They can use the land as they wish.' This article should not be considered as part of the treaty, yet no one brought up the issue and the Chinese government could not dare to mention it. During the fourth year of Emperor Tong Zhi (1865), the State Affairs department of the government issued an order: 'The churches in the inland area have been there for a long time. The properties the foreign missionaries have bought were used to build churches and the contracts involved should be protected by law. All others that were used for private purposes are forbidden by law and are prohibited. In the future, if any missionary wants to buy land to build churches should be granted permission. Do not get confused.'

Therefore, it became legal for the Catholic missionaries to buy or rent property for religious purposes.

2. Religious Orders Spread out in China

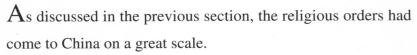

As discussed in the previous section, the religious orders had come to China on a great scale.

Let us take the Society of Jesuit as an example for the sake of discussion. In 1814, after the suppression of the Jesuits in the previous century, they were preparing to re-enter China. In 1840, Pope Gregory XVI sent Claudius Gottleland, and two other Jesuits (Ai Fangji and Li Xiufang) to the Jiangnan area. In 1846, When Emperor Dao Guang lifted the order on the Church's suppression, Gottleland began to talk with officials in Shanghai to regain church property. Since the old church in the city had been turned into a temple, the Jesuits were given three pieces of land in three different areas instead: namely, Dong Jiadu, Yang Jingbang and Shi Pinong. In 1861, because of the influence of the French military, the old church property and the residence of the priests were returned to the Jesuits. Xu Jia Hui was Xu Guangqi's hometown and his many descendants were Catholics who donated that piece of land to the Church. In 1847, the Jesuits set up their headquarters in Xu Jiahui, and Gottleland became the first rector. During the years of 1851 and 1853, the Cathedral in Dong Jiadu and a church in Xu Jiahui were erected.

In the 19th Century, the Jesuits built up many things in Xu Jiahui: seminary, library, natural museum (1869), observatory (1873), Newspaper Press of the Sacred Heart (1887), two convents for nuns, a refugee camp and a nursery. By 1890, there were 665 churches in the Jiangnan area, 77 small chapels, two seminaries and another one to train Chinese priests, one orphanage, one nursery and one hospital.

The Jesuits devoted themselves to education and built many schools in Shanghai. They had Xuhui Gong Xue and the Aloysius elementary school in Xu Jiahui alone. They accepted Catholic students to study not only the Catechism, but also Confucian Classics. By 1856, the Jesuits had 78 schools in Jiangnan area with 260 students. [1]

The missionaries of the Congregation of the Mission were spread out in Henan, Menggu, Zhejiang and Zhili provinces. In 1860, when the military of Britain and France occupied Beijing, they resumed missionary activities there. The Dominican Order was in Fujian province, Franciscans in Hunan, Hubei, Shanxi, Shaanxi and Shandong provinces; the Paris Foreign Mission sent

[1] Lai De Lie, Zhong Guo Ji Du Jiao Chuan Jiao Shi, Mai Ke Mi Lun Press, 1929, p236

priests to Sichuan, Yunnan and Guizhou, and eventually to Manchuria, Guangxi, Guangdong, Guizhou, Hainan and Tibet.

The second half of the 19th century of China was crowded with missionaries from all over the world. Some of the newly founded European religious orders tried to catch up with the older ones by sending more of their own to China. The most famous one was the Congregation of the Immaculate Heart of Mary founded in 1865 by Verbiest. He brought three priests from Belgium to China. A year later, they arrived at Da Xi Wan Zi to take the place of the Congregation of the Mission in Mongolia. They arrived in Gansu in 1878 and went to Xinjiang in 1884. With the expansion of activities, the Apostolic Vicariate was divided into three. There were 37 priests from this order and nine Chinese priests administering these places. [1] At the end of the century, there were 112 missionaries and 18 Chinese priests in total. They had boys' schools and girls' schools, and a seminary for training Chinese priests.

Following the coming of the missionaries, the Catholic Church was revitalized and further developed. By 1858, religious activities could be seen everywhere and the number of Catholics began to increase quickly. In 1870, there were 36,9411 Catholics [2] , in 1885 the number had reached 558,980, with 35

① Luo Guang (editor), Tian Zhu Jiao Zai Hua Chuan Jiao Shi Ji, Quang Qi Press, 1967, p188
② some other statistic was 404530

◎ Picture of the Episcopal ordination of Li Side and Jin Luxian of Shanghai diocese in 1984. This is the procession of the solemn celebration

bishops, 453 foreign missionaries and 273 Chinese priests. In 1890, the number of Catholics rose to 620,000, and by the 1897, there were 759 European missionaries and 409 Chinese priests. [1]

In order to adapt to the changes in China, Rome decided to reorganize the Apostolic Vicariates. In 1846, there were 10 dioceses in China, among which, three were archdioceses: Macao, Beijing and Nanjing; there were seven Apostolic Vicariates: Shaanxi, Shanxi, Shandong, Huguang, Jiangxi, Yunnan and Hong Kong.

① Lai Dei Lie, Zhong Guo Ji Du Jiao Chuan Jiao Shi, Mai Ke Mi Lun Press, 1929, p329

In 1870, Rome called a meeting in the Vatican and the majority of the Apostolic delegates in China attended to discuss affairs in China. They proposed to divide the country into five mission territories. Later, the missionary provinces would be built on this basis. In 1879 (5th year of Guang Xu), the mission territories were divided as follows: the first one included Zhili, Liaodong and Mongolia; the second included Shandong, Shaanxi, Henan, Gansu; the third included Hunan, Hubei, Zhejiang, Jiangxi and Jiangnan; the fourth included Sichuan, Yunnan, Guizhou and Tibet; the fifth included Guangdong, Guangxi, Hong Kong and Fujian. They decided that every territory should have a meeting every five years and the remaining territories needed to send representatives to participate. In 1880, the five missionary territories had their meetings separately mainly to discuss church affairs. They also talked about the administering of the sacraments, the training of Chinese priests and pastoral methodology.

Rome increased its financial support from 637,000 Francs a year in 1867 to 861,000 in 1882. This amount of money was only half of the entire cost of China operations, and the religious orders had to raise the rest on their own. Most of the money was raised in China. They rented out church property, except the use of the churches and areas like Shanghai, Tianjin and Sichuan did well in collecting rents. In 1877, when a terrible famine broke out in Northern China, the missionaries rented their lands to non-Catholics to earn interest.

3. Fifty Years of Religious Persecution

During the 19th century, the Catholic Church developed under
the protection of Western guns, yet, the persecution kept occurring and the Church, in a way, was in direct confrontation with
Chinese society. According to statistics, from 1856, when the
missionaries came back to China after the Opium War until 1899,
there were 1,500 reported incidents. The reason for this was that
the Western imperialists had invaded China in the name of religion, which offended the Chinese terribly. Meanwhile, some
missionaries were arrogant and acted as the agents of the Western imperialist invasion. They did many things harmful to the
Chinese: trying to collect vital military information, taking over
lands, acting as upholders of the law and cheating people. When
there were lawsuits involving Catholics, the local officials dared
not to offend the foreign missionaries and took the side of the
Catholics. Some people even became Catholics because they
wanted to win their lawsuits. One saying calling the Catholic
Church a 'church of lawsuits' was rather popular. In Songjiang,

Shanghai, another saying was widely spread among the people: 'No one enters the church unless there is lawsuit involved.' Worst of all, some criminals continued to do bad things after they became Catholics and were still protected by the missionaries.

The Xi Lin Persecution in 1856 was caused by Chapdeleine, a priest from the Paris Foreign Mission, who broke the law by entering the inland territories. Using this as an excuse, the French and British governments started the second Opium War. After the signing of the Zhong Fa Tianjin Treaty, Zhang Mingfeng was dismissed from office for good . All missionaries were allowed to go inland for religious purposes and were granted special favors. 'They were permitted to purchase land for their own purposes.'

Some missionaries greatly offended local people with their violation of the rules. A case in Qingyan, Guizhou in 1861 provides a perfect example. In April, after the bishop of Guizhou, Hu Fuli, received his passport issued by the French ambassador, he acted as a victor and was carried in a luxurious carrier along with many people to visit a local official. He forced people to sell land to him so that he could build a seminary and a printing press, causing great public offense. The officials, *Xunfu* He Guanying and *Tidu* (governor)Tian Xingshu sent a joint letter to the provincial government asking that the Catholic missionaries be expelled. On the feast of Duanwu (May 5th), the people set the seminary in Chaojiaguan on fire and killed four Catholics, one of whom was Zhang Ruyang. Bishop Hu Fuli reported to the French ambassador, resulting in another diplomatic confrontation. On the feast of Yuanxiao in the following year, the people in Kaizhou Jiasha tried to collect money to build a dragon lantern as an offering to the dragon-god according to custom, but the French missionary Wen Naier asked Chinese Catholics not to participate in this action. The governor Dai Luzhi ordered the arrest of Wen Naier and other four Chinese Catholics and executed them without delay. Because of this, Bishop Hu Fuli reported to the French embassy and the ambassador asked the Qing government to discipline the local officials by firing them. After negotiations, the Qing government caved in and sent all related officials into exile and paid 12,000 pieces of silver in compensation.

Sichuan was another place where religious persecution happened frequently, of which the 'Youyang Persecution' was a particular case. In 1865, Zhang Peichao and his son Zhang Yuguan were angry with some Chinese Catholics and burned down churches, killed missionaries and wrote slogans such as 'destroy and uproot the foreign church'. In 1869, another Catholic whose name was Long Xiuyuan forced a non-Catholic Zhu Yongtai to break a marriage vow and caused another fight between Catholics and non-Catholics. The local officials ordered the two parties to turn in their weapons to the government. The non-Catholics did so, but the Catholics refused to obey the order. Under the leadership of a Chinese priest Tan Fuchen, 200 non-Catholics were killed. The government, however, paid 30,000 pieces of silver to settle the case and then killed the leader of the non-Catholics and others; those who weren't killed were expelled. Father Tan and the bishop left the country, while the lay people involved went free.

Shortly after that, the anti-church movement gained momentum along both sides of the Yangtze River. Anti-church slogans appeared everywhere in Hunan province: 'all the people, no matter the scholars, peasants, workers and the business people should be united to attack them.' Soon after, many churches were destroyed and the unrest spread as far as Yangzhou. Eventually, the French ambassador sent military gunboats to Hankou, and to Anqing to suppress the uprisings. Meanwhile, other anti-church movements broke out in many places: Yongning in Guizhou Province, Fuzhou in Fujian Province, Zhangpu, Luoyuan, Leizhou in

◎ Catholic church in Tianjin

Guangdong Province, for example.

Another religious persecution occurred in Tianjin. In 1870, French missionaries built an orphanage called Ren Ci Tang at the East Gate of Tianjin. All the orphans in the orphanage were baptized. A suspected child-kidnaper whose name was Wu Lanzhen was arrested and admitted that the gatekeeper at the orphanage had asked him to do so. He went out to kidnap seven children during daytime. Immediately, the rumor spread that the church kidnapped the children to use their eyes for medicine, provoking riots.

On June 21, officials in Tianjin, Zhou Xunguang, Zhang Guangcao and Liu Jie, took Wu Lanzhen to the church to see the priest Xie Fuyin. In the afternoon, the people who were there had an argument with some church members that led to violence. Some five people went to the French embassy to argue with officials, and Feng Daye thought that what was happening was due to local officials not making efforts to protect Catholics. He went to the government office with two guns and his secretary Simon followed him with a sword in his hand.[1] After he arrived at the government office, he was very rude and knocked on the table using his sword, screaming at Chong Hou: 'Those crazy people want to kill me and I want you to die in front of me.' He fired his gun and wounded several people. Many members of Shui Huo Hui (Water and Fire Gang) gathered outside of the office while this was going on. Chong Hou asked them not to

① From Zhong Guo first History achieve, Qing Mo Jiao An, Zhong Hua Shu Ju, 1996, p776 go out of the office for their safety. Feng Daye refused to listen and said, 'I am not afraid of the Chinese people.' On his way back, he met the local governor Liu Jie returning from the local church. They argued to the point of violence. Some people were hurt and the secretary Simon fired at the people twice. The Chinese were furious about this and killed Feng Daye and Simon and threw their bodies into the river. Afterwards, a mob gathered to burn down the churches, Renci Tang, and the French Consulate; they killed the missionaries, business people and Chinese Catholics, including priests and church workers. This violence did not end until five o'clock in the afternoon. Besides the attacks on the French, the Chinese also burned down the churches that had been built by Britain and USA.

Many non-Chinese died during this religious persecution, including the French missionary Xie Fuyin, a couple who were the consulate's translators, a French business couple Sha Er Mei Song, Russian businessman Ba Suofu , Robert Pin Pin Fu and his wife, ten nuns from France, Russia, Belgium, Italy, Ireland and another 20 people.

After the Tianjin Persecution, the ambassadors from more than seven countries including Britain, the United States, France, Belgium and Russia issued a joint letter to require a meeting with Yixin and sent their military boats to Haikou, Tianjin and Yantai, Shandong Province, to demonstrate their military strength. On June 23, Chong Hu reported the Tianjin incident to the Emperor, and the government sensed the severity of matter and asked Zeng Guofang to investigate it the following day. On the 25th, Emperor Tong Zhi decided to arrest the leaders, Chong Hou, Zhou Jiaxun, Zhang Guangcao and Liu Jie, and sent them to different courts for punishment. On the 28th, he ordered not to follow Tianjin's example in persecuting. On September 12th, he sent Li Hongzhang to Tianjin 'to meet Zeng Guofang, Ding Richang and Cheng Lin to solve the problem as soon as possible.'

On October 5th, Emperor Tong Zhi ordered: 'Because the people in Tianjin gathered to cause trouble and some gangsters snuck into the crowds, many innocent people were killed. The criminals are still at large. This is a very serious matter...Therefore, Zhang Guangcao, Liu Jie and others should be sent into exile in Heilongjiang Province.' [①] Two groups of people who participated in this religious persecution were executed separately, including 20 common people and 25 soldiers. On the request of France, China paid 210,000 Pieces of silver for the damage done to the embassies, churches and Ci Ren Tang, etc. and 250,000

① From Zhong Guo first History achieve, Qing Mo Jiao An, Zhong Hua Shu Ju, 1996, p933

Pieces of Silver to console the victims. Chong Hou was sent to France on China's behalf to apologize.

Tianjin Religious Persecution was a voluntary anti-imperialist movement from the people which inspired many others nationwide. The Anti-foreign church movement was not stopped by the cruelty of the feudalistic government; on the contrary, it became more violent. In the Spring of 1873, Joseph Fan, the bishop of Chuandong, sent Father Yu Kelan to Qianjiang County to buy houses with the intension to build a local church. In August, French missionary Yu Kelin and Chinese priest Dai Mingqin were bitten to death by the local people. French government once again asked for compensation. The result of this case was that two leaders were executed and China paid 40,000 Francs for reparations. This kind of anti-church movement kept occurring in Sichuan, Xanchong, Yingshang, Linshui, Jiangbeiting, Neishan and Peizhou, and many churches, priests' residences and lay people's houses were burned down.

Later, Shandong, Fujian, Guangdong, Guangxi, Xizang, Yunnan, Taiwan, Zhejiang, Sichuan, Anhui, Jiangsu, Hunan and Heilongjiang provinces had similar confrontations between churches and local people, though on different scales. The worst ones were in Dazu in Sichuan Province, Wuhu in Anhui Province and in Juye in Shandong Province.

The Qing government realized the severity of such confrontations and the Zongli Yamen (State Council) decided to draft a law 'Chuan Jiao Zhang Cheng'(Constitution of Missions) in 1871, but this was rejected by the European countries. In the following years, Guo Sontao in 1876, Li Hongzhang in 1892 and Yu Deti in 1897 suggested the same rules in order to stop the confrontations between the local people and the churches, but they all failed. In 1899 (the 25th year of Guang Xu), the Zongli Yamen issued a law in order for local government leaders to accept the missionaries. Though the combination of politics and missionary works was strange enough in the feudalistic cultural atmosphere, some missionaries still liked this legal protection and some even enjoyed traveling in the official costumes.

The Qing government was too kind to the strong European countries and to the missionaries, while treating its own people very differently. Whenever religious persecution started, the policy of 'Bu Ren Min Jiao, Dan fen Liang You' (no matter local people or the church, as long as the party is in good standing) would become 'Bu Fen Lian You, Dan Feng Min Jiao' (No matter which party is good, as long as you distinguish who is who). This government's action greatly offended the people. In 1894, the Sino-Japanese war broke out leading to Chinese defeat. In April 1895, the Treaty of Portsmouth was signed and patriotism and the anti-church movement once again peaked in China.

Another anti-imperialism and patriotic movement broke out in 1900, which was called Yi He Tuan Movement (Boxer Rebellion). Most of the members were farmers, peasants and the jobless. They hated Westerners and were rather patriotic. They had a slogan 'Destroy the Westerners and safeguard the Qing Dynasty'. As a secretive group, they certainly had their own superstitious ideas and xenophobic feelings; therefore, they hated anything that was foreign to them, including the Catholic Church. They thought all the natural disasters and social problems were caused by the foreign church. The anti-imperialist and anti-church movement was countered by the creation of an eight-nation Western alliance in Tianjin in June to attack Beijing. On the 21st, the Qing government decided to declare war against the eight countries and encouraged the Yi He Tuan (Boxers) to resist the foreigners. As rapid as fire, the movement spread from Tianjin and Beijing to Liaoning, Heilongjiang, Yunnan, Guizhou, Hebei, Shanxi, Shaanxi and Sichuan provinces.

Overall, the Catholic Church suffered terribly because of the Boxer Rebellion. Statistically, five bishops, 31 European priests and nine nuns were killed.[①] More 30,000 Chinese Catholics were killed and about three-quarters of the Catholic churches were destroyed. In some places, the church organizations were nearly wiped out.

① Lai Lai Dei Lie, Zhong Guo Ji Du Jiao Chuan Jiao Shi, Mai Ke Mi Lun Press, 1929, p512

4. Catholic Church in the first half of the 20th Century

After the defeat of the Boxer Rebellion, the Qing government decided to lay out rules to protect the church all over China. The largest reparation in modern Chinese history is the 'Geng Zi Reparation'. Part of the money was used to rebuild the destroyed and damaged churches, as well as new ones. The officials implicated in the religious persecution numbered well over 50. In 1911, the Qing Dynasty was overthrown and religious freedom was included in the new constitution of the Republic of China. The separation of Church and State was clearly stated and all religions were protected by law. The social changes in China made it reasonable for the Catholic Church to recover and to develop further. In the meantime, it also made some changes by barring missionaries from getting directly involved in politics and interfering with people's lawsuits. The Church began to concentrate on providing various social services.

A. Number of Catholics kept increasing

From 1901 to 1910, church membership increased from 720,540 to 1,364,618. According to the 1920 statistics on Christians in China from the China Xu Xing Committee, the number of Catholics increased to 1,971,189 and kept growing. By 1940, there were 3,183,000 Catholics and, this number kept steady until 1949.

B. Religious Orders in China kept increasing

The main religious orders in China were the Salesians of Don Bosco, the Order of St. Augustine, the Yisudeng Foreign Mission, St. Columban Foreign Mission, the Congregation of the Passion, Congregation of Sacred Hearts Mary and Jesus, Congregation of the Sacred Heart, Order of St. Benedict, etc.. Besides these male groups, there were many female religious orders as well, such as the Franciscan Missionaries of Mary, Little Sisters of the Poor, Missionary Sisters of Our Lady of the Angles, etc.. During the First World War, many Western countries were distracted by the combat so that the number of missionaries became less and the amount of the money to support the missions was reduced. After the war, the American economy developed quickly and Americans became involved with missionary work in China. In 1918, the Maryknoll missionaries came to Jiangmei

◎ A Chinese Style Catholic church in Hanzhong which was built at the beginning of the 20th century

in Guangdong Province under the leadership of Thomas Pulleys. He became the head of this Apostolic Vicariate in 1925. Other American religious orders like the Columban Fathers, Congregation of the Mission, Passionist Fathers, Divine Word Fathers, came to China.

C. Catholic Church intensified missionary work

In 1908, the Roman Curia re-emphasized its orders not to allow missionaries in China to get involved with private lawsuits and not to get involved in politics and diplomatic matters.

Because of this, the so-called Da Guansi Jiao (the Church that is involved with lawsuits) image began to decline. The Church began to concentrate on improving Chinese Catholics' morale that also influenced others. The Congregation of the Faith in Rome forbade Catholics from smoking opium, as well as not allowing Catholics to sell their wives or daughters for economic reasons. Whoever did this would not be allowed to receive the sacrament. The missionaries also helped to change the bad old customs, of marrying young or having a Tong Yong Xi (a fixed marriage in which the women is much older). The missionaries also helped farmers to improve their skills and the irrigation sys-

◎ A mission church in Hanzhong which was built at the beginning of the 20th century

tem.

The Church began to value the quality of the Catholics rather than merely quantity. For those wanting to join the Church there was a two-year probation period according to the rules of the Jesuits, Divine Word Fathers and Congregation of the Immaculate Heart of Mary. Some local churches even set aside money to attract catechists. In Beijing Diocese, for instance, every missionary could receive six dollars for each convert. Simply because of this, a folk saying, Chijiao (eat what the church provides), emerged.

D. Social Services development

Among all the charitable organizations of the Church, orphanages were the most important. The number of orphans and abandoned children that they received indeed increased the number of baptisms. The Catholic Church believed that a baptized infant could go to heaven directly. If the infants survived, they would grow up as Catholics. Yuying Tang (house for infants) was usually a part of an orphanage. All the children sent to Yuying Tang, were barely alive. The death rate was extremely high, most of them died rather quickly after baptism.

The orphanage and the Yuying Tang were well developed

◎ The picture of all the orphans in the orphanage run by Nuns

in the 20th century. In 1920, there were 150 orphanages in China, with 20 in Zhili, 21 in Jiangsu, 14 in Zhejiang, 13 in Guangdong and 10 in Menggu. Overall, they housed some 17,000 orphans. By 1930, the number increased to 375 orphanages [①] with 21,858 orphans. In Fujian Province alone, there were 13 orphanages with 15,000 children, of whom 500 stayed in regular families. The church taught boys basic skills in business and girls domestic skills. Most of them were baptized and were part of Catholic families when they grew up. In fact, the Catholics coming from orphanages occupied a rather high percentage of church membership. The biggest Catholic church in Shanghai, Xu Jiahui,

① Ding Ru Ren, Quang Guo Jiao Wu Qing Xing zhi Hui Gu, from Sheng Jiao Za Zhi, vol.5, 1931

had a quarter of its congregation who came from orphanages in Tushangwang and the Blessed Mother Orphanages. [1] When they were still very young, they learned prayers and studied the catechism under the strict supervision of the priests and nuns. They also had to attend to religious activities. When they reach the age of marriage, the priests in Tushanwan and the sisters from the house would help arrange a partner. Usually, the boys and girls from orphanages would be matched. After they received the nuptial blessing from the priests in the church, they could move into a house provided by the church. [2]

Clinics and hospitals were another charitable work and were important to the Church mission in China. At the beginning of the 20th century, the most famous Catholic hospitals in China were the French Hospital established in Kunming in 1901. the Caritas Hospital in Chongqing and the Taomei Hospital in Guangzhou in 1905, a French Hospital in Qingdao in 1906 the Guangci Hospital in Shanghai in 1907, the French Women's and Children's Hospital in Nanchang in 1929 and the Puci Sanatorium in Shanghai in 1935. Father Kong Haogu built another hospital for lepers in Guangzhou and another hospital specialized in curing rat pestilence in Manchu. By 1937, the French Catholic Church alone had established 70 hospitals with 5,000 beds. [3]

[1] Gu Yu Lu, Zhong Guo Tian Zhu Jiao de Guo Qu he Xian Zai, Shanghai Social Science Institute press,1989. p62
[2] Gu Yu Lu, Xu Jia Hui Tian Zhu Tang de Guo Qu he Xian Zai, from Zong Jiao Wen Ti TanSuo-1984),p174
[3] Gu Wei Min, Ji Du Jiao yu Xian dai Zhong Guo She Hui), p389

◎ Catholic priest baptizing Chinese babies at the beginning of the 20th century

Objectively speaking, besides expanding church influence in China, the purpose of establishing hospitals was to introduce medical scientific theories for hospital management and medical education etc. They trained many doctors in Western medicine for China, which was another great contribution.

The nursing home was another service the Catholic Church provided. There were 37 nursing homes in China in 1920 with the average of 35 people in each. The ones who provided services to the elderly people were nuns from the Little Sisters of the Poor. The number of nursing homes reached 232 in 1930.

The Social Services of the Catholic Church included another well-organized economic branch. From 1876 to 1879, rare severe natural disasters occurred in Shandong, Zhili, Shanxi, Shaanxi and Henan provinces. The Catholic Church sent some 70 missionaries to the affected places to help. Certainly some used the opportunity to buy land and later rented them to the peasants on the condition of becoming Catholics. Most of them were there to help, however. Whenever a disaster occurred, they were there to help out, which won the hearts of many and therefore strengthened and expanded the Catholic Church. For instance, when the northern part of China was flooded in 1931, the Catholic Church alone contributed 200,000 Yuan to help the victims.

E. Educational expansion

Since the 19th century, the Catholics valued basic education in two main forms, general education and catechetical education. The Church used the Gen Zi Pei Kuan (indemnity money) to build and develop many junior and senior schools. The teachers were either local well-educated lay people or priests who taught the Catholic children their catechism, Chinese, all kinds of prayers and basic readings and writings. The students were mainly Catholics, but the schools also accepted non-Catholic students.

The junior school was mainly designed to teach Catholics the Catechism in order to help them to deepen their understanding of the doctrine and strengthen their faith. In 1914, the Catholic Church was running 8,034 schools with a student population of 132,850. Most of these students were in junior schools.[1] By 1925 when the Catholic congregation reached 2,500,000, there were 310,000 students in the schools. In fact, two-third of the schools were teaching Catholic doctrine.[2] In general, each vicariate had at least one seminary. There were 64 Catholic seminaries in 1906 with 1,640 students.

In terms of higher education, the Catholic Church lagged behind the Protestant Church, and yet the efforts the local churches made were obvious to all. In 1908, a vocational school in central Mongolia began to teach Western subjects. In 1908, a Catholic vocational school began to teach English and French. St. Joseph's College in Fuzhou was the only local higher educational institution.

In March of 1903, Ma Xiangbo, a well-known Catholic scholar, established Zhen Dan (Aurora) University in Xu Jiahui with the intention of revitalizing Chinese culture via higher education. Because of the interference of a French Jesuit priest Nan Congzhou, Ma Xiangbo left the university. With the help of some

[1] Lin Zhiping (editor), Jin Dai Zhong Guo yu Ji Du Jiao Lun Wen Ji, p138
[2] The general education, the effort that the Protestant Church was made seemly exceeded the Catholic Church's. the schools that the Protestant Church built were over 4100 which was half the Catholic ones, but the student enrollment was over 11300. which was equivalent with the Catholic ones

other patriotic scholars, however, he founded Fu Dan Gong Xu in Li Gongsi, Xu Jiahui in 1905. In 1908, Zhen Dan University moved to the French section and the Jesuit priest Nan Congzhou became its president. This school used French to teach the courses in literature, law, natural sciences and engineering, as well as medicine. Most of the professors were Jesuit priests. Moreover, this was a boys' school. Zhen Dan was a pontifical university under the supervision of the Congregation of Faith in Rome. In 1932, it officially registered as Zhen Dan University. In 1935, it had a law, medical and business school. It offered a four-year

◎ The Cathedral of Guangzhou diocese which is located at the center of the city. It is called Shi Shi Jiao Tang. This cathedral was began on June 18th , 1863 and was finished in 1888

program, except for the medical school, which was six years. By 1936, Zhen Dan had 300 undergraduates, and a preparatory school had another 300 students. A women's college was established in 1938. In 1922, the Jesuits established another university in Tianjin, which was called Jin Gu Da Xue. This had schools of business and commerce. The university then began to recruit the preparatory students. In March 1923, they recruited 50 students and in 1933, it changed its name to Tian Jing Gong Shang Xueyuan.

In November of 1917, Ying Lianzhi (1867-1926), a Chinese Catholic, and Ma Xiangbo wrote a joint letter to Pope Pius X asking for permission to establish a university, and gained his approval along with some funding. The Pope asked Dr. O'Toole, an American Benedictine who held doctoral degrees in theology and philosophy, to travel to China to discuss the matter. In 1922, the Pope personally donated 100,000 Lira to start with. The American Benedictines were asked to take charge of the university and Mr. McManus provided $100,000 as foundation capital. On October 1, 1925, Fu Ren University was officially established with a School of Arts and Letters, School of Natural Sciences and School of Education with an enrollment of about 500 students. In the overworking second year of its establishment,

Ying Lianzhi died of overworking. After that, Chen Yuan, a well-known historian, became the president.

F. Media expansion

By 1920, the Catholic Church had 13 printing presses, such as those in Hong Kong, Shanghai, Beijing and Hebei Province. They printed many Catholic and non-Catholic works in many languages. There were 15 Catholic periodicals, the most famous being Sheng Jiao Magazine, printed in Shanghai; Yi Shi Bo, founded by the Belgium priest Lebbe in October 1915 in Tianjin. *Sheng Jiao Magazine* was very religious and the articles tended to be in a series. The 12th generation descendent of Xu Guangqi, Xu Zongze became its editor in 1923 and the magazine began to discuss social issues. [1] Yi Shi Bo, however, was rather political from the beginning. Since Japan has forced China to sign the 21 Demands, the magazine began to inspire people's sense of nationalism in order to save the country. It had tremendous influence. Lebbe was praised and honored by the government.

There were 14 Catholic printing presses in 1926 publishing 15 journals of which nine were in French, three in Chinese, one in Portuguese, one in English and one in Latin. In 1930, there were 20 printing presses with 30 journals of various types. In

[1]　Yuan Ren Ze, Gao Zhen Nong (editors), Shanghai Zongjiao Shi, p712-714

1928, the *Zhong Huo Gongjiao Jiaoyu Lianhehui* (Chinese Catholic Education Association) was founded in Beijing to oversee all the publications. This association was headed by the Apostolic delegate with a monthly publication *Zhonghua Gongjiao Jiaoyu Lianhehuai Congkan* (Chinese Catholic Education Association Series). It was published in Chinese, Latin, English and French. [①]

① De Li Xian, Zhong Guo Tian Zhu Jiao Chuan Jiao Shi, p102

5. Relationship Between the Vatican and China

At the end of the 19th century, the Qing Emperor tried on numerous occasions to bypass France to establish diplomatic relations with the Vatican, but this always foundered on French opposition. At the beginning of the 20th century, the government resumed dialogue with the Vatican to establish a normal relations. In November 1914, Pope Pius XV sent his regards to Yuan

© Apostolic Delegate in China
Constantini(1876 — 1958)

Shikai via the Apostolic Delegate in Beijing. In 1918, the foreign minister Lu Chengxiang, who was a Catholic, tried to contact Rome to establish direct diplomatic relations. On July 11, 1918, the Vatican released an announcement in the official newspaper L'Observatore Romano that it intended to send a papal delegate to China. But this idea was dropped again due to

French opposition.

After the May 4th Movement in 1919, Chinese Catholics became rather enthusiastic to build up the church. Rome made certain adaptations to make the Church more Chinese. Once again, the Government resumed diplomatic contacts. In 1922, Rome sent Bishop Celso Constantini as the Apostolic Delegate to China. In November, he arrived in Hong Kong and on New Year's Day 1923, he arrived at Beijing to meet President Li Yuanhong. Constantini's residence was set up temporarily in Wuhan and in 1928 was officially moved to Gong Wang Fu in Beijing. On October 1, 1923, Pope Pius XI recognized the Nanjing Government in a telegram. On January 22, 1929, Constantini was invited to meet Chiang Kaishek, but, in 1933, he returned to Italy for health reasons. Archbishop Zaning (1890-1958) succeeded him.

Sending the Apostolic Delegate to China ended France's power to overshadow Rome, however, the development of the diplomatic relations did not run smoothly. The Vatican publicly recognized the state of Manchukuo established by the Imperialist Japanese. In February, it named the Bishop of Jilin, a priest from the Parish Foreign Mission, to be the Apostolic Delegate to Manchukuo, which became a diocese in its own right separate from China. In September 1938, Pope Pius XI received church representatives from Manchukuo and wrote to Emperor Pu Yi. In February 1939, the newly elected Pope XII wrote to Pu Yi reaffirming Rome's stance. On March 12th, the Chinese government sent a special envoy Gu Weijun to Rome to attend the consecration of Pius XII, but he made no criticism of the Japanese invasion of China as was hoped. Archbishop Zannini sent a pastoral letter to Chinese Catholics asking them to be neutral on the Japanese invasion, 'Be wise and patient, concentrating on holy things and not politically oriented. Try to avoid any expressional support.' Until 1942, Rome resisted pressure to abandon its diplomatic ties with Japan.

The actions of the Rome and the Apostolic Delegate offended the Chinese including many Catholics. The Chinese government tried to use diplomatic channels to ask Rome to take the China side even though the Archbishop's pastoral letter was voicing opposite opinions. From the September 18th Incident in 1931, when the Japanese occupied the three provinces of Northeast China until July 7, 1937, when war was declared throughout China, the whole nation's destiny worried all patriotic people. Most Catholics shared the same feelings as the rest of the country that the nation was in trouble and every citizen had a duty to safeguard it. Many well-known people, such as Ma Xiangbo, Lu Chengxiang and Yu Bin expressed their support for China to resist the foreign invasion. While at an advanced age of 92, Ma Xiangbo wrote an article *Ri Huo Jing Gao Guo Ren Shu* (Letter to remind all people about Japanese's crimes)to call on all people in China to be united to save the nation. In December, he wrote *Qi Gao Qingnian Shu* (Letter to the Youth with tears)to call on the youth to go to the countryside to persuade them to standup for China. In January 1932, he wrote *Xin Nian Gao Qing Nian Shou* (Letter to the youth on New Year's Day) asking the young people to boycott Japanese products. Meanwhile, he encouraged them to study science in order to build up and strengthen the country. The Apostolic Delegate, who was in the northwest on a pastoral visit, went to Hankou and sent a pastoral letter asking the Catholic Church to do more in regard to charitable works in wartime. He also celebrated Mass for victims of the war. Many patriotic Catholics donated money or clothing to the soldiers in the frontline; some even formed a emergency medical team to go with the military. Many missionaries in Manchukuo also secretly helped the anti-Japanese movement; some even protected the anti-Japanese leaders in their houses. The Chinese Communist Party established its government in Wan

Pin County in 1938 and Father Zhao was elected as a member of the council. He received many local and military officials in his church and had a medical team to help wounded soldiers.

A year after establishing diplomatic relations with Japan, Rome had also official diplomatic relations with the Republic of China in June of 1943. In July, Xie Shoukang was named as the first ambassador to Rome. The Vatican, however, did not send a delegate to China until 1946 when Archbishop Ribeiri, a Moroccan, was named the Apostolic Nuncio to China. When Xie Shoukang retired from his post in 1946, Wu Jingxiong, a Catholic scholar took over. In June 1949, Wu left his post for the US and Zhu Ying went to Rome in his place.

The hierarchical system was officially implemented in April 1946. There were 20 provinces and each province had an archbishop. There were 79 dioceses; each diocese should have had a bishop. By 1948, out of the 20 provinces, there were 84 dioceses and 35 administrative regions.

6. Chinese Catholics' Patriotic Movement

Upon entering the 20th century, the Chinese people's national-istic and patriotic sentiments became stronger, the anti-imperi-alist and democratic movement was raised to a new level; many Catholics felt the urgency of joining the rest of the country to fight against the foreigners. In the way, they called for Church independence.

As early as 1917, the well-known patriotic Catholic Yin Lianzhi wrote an Exhortation to Study in which he criticized the missionaries' hypocrisy: 'Do not missionaries everywhere sing the praises of their respective countries of France, Italy and Ger-many?' 'Their zeal is satisfied only when they have succeeded in making submissive subjects for their own countries out of the Catholics of our China.' After the May 4th Movement appeared, many Catholics and young students from Catholic schools joined the anti-imperialist and patriotic movements. The Student Com-mittee from Zhen Dan University, and the students from the Sino-French school in Shanghai, Xu Jia Hui Catholic School and from many other schools staged 'three-phase strikes' (no work, no school no marketing). Moreover, students from Catholic schools in Tianjin, Beijing and Guangzhou also participated in the Anti-Imperialist War. Patriotic Catholics in Tianjin formed a Catholic Salvation Unit and joined with other social classes to form an association. They went out to give lectures on patriotism. They sent flyers and a declaration to Catholics everywhere. In the November 6 issue of Yi Shi Bao, they published an

◎ On April 3rd, 1994, Easter Sunday, there were about 3000 Catholics from Both China and abroad gathered at Xuan Wu Men Cathedral for the Celebration. The Picture is a non Non-Chinese who receives Communion

article in which they called on all Catholics to 'rise up, safeguard our country...giving a hand to the nation.' On June 12th, Nie Xingwu, a Catholic who wrote an article *Wei wai Jiao Qi Gao Jiao Zhong Ren Shu* (Letter to the catholics for diplamatic

Reasons) for *Yi Shi Bao* in which he pointed out that the Western countries had invaded China in the name of religion. 'Whenever there is religious persecution, we either lose power or lose land and our country is losing followed by evangelization''. *Sheng Jiao Magazine*, run by the Jesuits, also published an article Gong *Jiao You Zhi Re Xin Jiu Guo* (Catholics shuld devote yourselves to save the nation), which echoed Tianjin's patriotic movement, saying: 'This article is to encourage Catholics to rise up to save our country.'

Soon after the Chinese Catholics began showing their patriotism and loyalty towards China, some local church leaders criticized this very action. One month after *Sheng Jiao Magazine* expressed its opinion, some leaders made a Special Statement saying that Tianjin Catholics had 'falsely accused the clergy' and were 'denying the church'.

The statement also mentioned the Catholics 'seizing a pretext to attack the church leaders,' and they 'need to be punished'. From November 16th to 23rd, Guang Ruohang, the Bishop of Guangdong was hosting a meeting for bishops in Beijing, who in the name of the Apostolic Delegate, issued a letter To Priests in Zhi Li Province stating that the Church authority refused to have a Chinese Catholic Church. The 20th century was a time when Chinese nationalism became rather strong, and therefore, the Church authority's pressure on patriotic Catholics could only widen the gap between them.

Ying Lianzhi and Ma Xiangbo were the famous personages in the patriotic movement. Ying Lianzhi (1867-1926) was a Manchurian. At age of 19, he began to read Adam Schall's work *Zhu Zhi Qun Zheng* and became a Catholic when he was 22. In 1902, in order to help save China, he and his friends established the newspaper *Da Gong Bao*. He was unhappy to see the Catholic Church in China being dominated by foreigners and called for the training of good and excellent Chinese clergy. He was angry to see that the missionaries allowed themselves to love their own countries, while forbidding the Chinese Catholics to be patriotic. In his Exhortation to Study, he wrote: 'Recently, after the invasion of Belgium by Germany, Cardinal Mercier published a celebrated pastoral on Patriotism-love of the native soil, of the country of one's fathers--such was the theme that he developed in the document wherein the clearness of exposition is on a par with the nobility of the doctrine expounded, and all accordingly, both learned and ignorant, have been moved by it to the very depth of their souls. As for China, I vainly rack my memory in order to recall ever having heard a missionary exalt patriotism. Does this mean that the Catholic Church exacts from the Catholics of China alone the duty of loving the foreign countries rather than their own?' [①] He expressed his strong national pride and patriotic sentiment in his work. In 1926, this well-known scholar died with both great hope and profound regret.

Ma Xiangbo (1840-1939), a native of Danyang, Jiangsu Province, was born into an Catholic family and was baptized as Joseph. He took another name Hua Feng Lao Ren when he was advanced in years. He entered Saint Ignatius School when he was 12 to study Latin, French, mathematics, astronomy and religion. He joined the Jesuits in 1861 and was ordained to the priesthood in 1870. He began his mission in Xuancheng, Anhui Province and Nanjing and Xuzhou, Jiangsu Province. He left the priesthood in 1876 and married. He came back to work for the Church in 1898. After a year-long retreat in Sheshang, he received dispensation from the Holy Father. In 1903, he founded Zhen Dan University (Aurora) and in 1905 he founded Fu Dan Public School, meaning Recovering Zhen Dan. He retired in Xu Jiahui in 1920 concentrating on translating and writing books. Ma was a Catholic who was filled with nationalism and patriotism. He was saddened to see the Church affairs run by foreigners and the pressure that Chinese clergy had to endure from for-

① Ying Lian Zhi, Quan Xue Zui Yan, p4. It is taken from Gu Yu Lu, Zhong Guo Tian zhu Jiao de Guo Qu he Xian Zai, Shansaghai Social Sciences Institute press, 1989, p81

95

eigners. He strongly promoted the self-administration of the Catholic Church in China and the training of native priests and the need to improve the quality of missionary work and its social effect. After the 9.18 Incident in 1931, Ma Xiangbo, who was then in his 90s, showed his patriotism through his continued writings and lectures calling on all people to save China. He also wrote *Huan Wo He Shan* (Return our Land) calling for a halt to the Civil War in order to resist the Japanese solely. He proactively organized different associations to try to save China. He and Song Qingling organized a *Zhong Guo Min Quan Baozhang Tong Meng Hui* (Association for protecting Chinese People's Rights) in 1932. In 1935, other scholars, such as Shen Junyu and Zou Taofen organized *Jiu Guo Hui* (Saving China Association), with Ma Xiangbo, the most respected man, elected as president. In Jiu Wang Bao, dated July 12th 1936, Ma openly criticized the Nationalist government's non-resistance policy toward the Japanese. He said: 'Japan only has 80 million people and China has 400 million. Japan's population is only one fifth of China. How can such a huge country not resist small Japan's invasion? This is called Suo Tou Wu Gui (a Turtle with its Head hidden inside its Shell). This Suo Tou Wu Gui is the government, not the people. Even when the people tried to stand up to fight, the government tried to suppress it.' These rather patriotic speeches enhanced the Anti-Japanese Movement and influenced greatly the unification of the Chinese people. He was regard as a patriotic legend. When he had his centenary celebration in 1936, the Communist Party sent a telegram to congratulate him, saying, Light of the Nation, Auspice of Humanity. The Nationalist Government also praised him, calling him as a Hero of the Peoples, Auspice of the Nation. On November 4th, he died of illness in Vietnam. Mao Zedong, Zhu De and Peng Dehuai sent condolences to his family via telegram [1] in which they highly praised his lifetime's work.

① On November 10th, 1939, Xin Hua Daily in Chongqing reported the whole content

7. Efforts made in the Church's Enculturation

Enculturation is always an issue when a religion is introduced from one culture to another one, and Catholicism was no exception. The enculturation of the Catholic Church in China covered many areas: seminary education, Chinese liturgy, Chinese Bible, the translation of many Catholic classics, and the training of native Chinese priests. Certainly, this latter issue was the crucial one. The enculturation of the Catholic Church in China followed a long and tortuous path. During the first half of the 20th century, the Catholic Church made some progresses in the enculturation process; yet, it did not go too far. The Church was mostly dominated by non-Chinese clergy and foreign powers, and most of Chinese clergy and lay people were powerless.

After the Opium War, though only a few Chinese priests were in charge of church affairs, helping to solve the cultural and political problems, as well as the conversion of the people, they all did wonderfully well. According to the statistics, the number of priests was as follows: in 1903, there were 1,075 non-

Chinese priests and 499 Chinese priests; in 1912, the ratio was 1,469 to 729[1]; from 1919-1920, 1,417[2] to 863[3]; in 1940, 4,552 to 1,989; finally, in 1949, there were 6,024 non-Chinese and 2,155 Chinese priests[4]. Bishops were even rarer. For over 240 years, from when Matteo Ricci came to Guangdong in 1583, until 1926, there was only one native Chinese Bishop, Luo Wen Cao, and the remainder were all foreigners.

Though some hierarchy within the church were not in favor of Catholics being involved in the patriotic movement, and resisted the Church's enculturation, it was, in fact, unstoppable. The percentage of the native Chinese priests was increasing: in 1924, there were 834 Chinese priests, which was 35% of the total number, and in 1923, there 1,088 or 41%, and this percent-

① Lai De Lie, Zhong Guo Ji Du Jiao Chuan Jiao Shi, Mai Ke Mi Lun Press, 1929, p538
② Another statistics: in 1920, there were 6,204 Foreign priests and 1,308 Chinese priests. The ratio for the Chinese was even smaller. Cf. Li Kuan Shu, Zhog Guo Ji Du Jiao Shi Lue, China Social Science Institute press, 1998, p253
③ Ren Yan Li (editor), Zhong Guo Tian Zhu Jiao Ji Chu Zhi Shi, Religious culture press, 1999, p279
④ Li Kuan Shu, Zhong Guo Ji Du Jiao Shi Lue, China Social Science Institute press, 1998, p253

age remained in 1926. Many people in the Mongolia and Hankou dioceses began to sing the psalms to Chinese melodies when they attended Mass. During the period from 1920 to 1924, many Apostolic Vicariates began to name the dioceses by using the local cities' names, such as Tianjin Diocese.

A Chinese hierarchy was officially established in 1946 and the Catholic Church in China came under the Congregation of the Propagation of the Faith. China was divided into 20 provinces and each province had an archbishop. Among those 20 archbishops, there were 17 non-Chinese and three native Chinese. Those three were Tian Gengxin, Archbishop of Beijing Diocese who was named as the first Cardinal in February 1945, Archbishop Yu Bin of the Nanjing Diocese and Archbishop Zhou Jishi of the Nanchang Diocese. Under the provinces, there were 135 dioceses with only 14 native Chinese bishops. The ratio of native Chinese priests was no better either, for, although the number kept increasing, it never reached 50 percent of the total. From 1928 to 1929, there were 1,536 Chinese priests and there 2,015 non-Chinese, or 43%. In 1936, when the number of Chinese priests increased to 1,835, there were 2,717 non-Chinese for a lower ratio of 40%.

◎ Scene of the celebration of the feast of the Pentecost in Taiyuan, Shanxi Province

THE CATHOLIC THREE
CHURCH AFTER THE FOUNDING OF PRC

1. Imperialistic elements within the Church and the New China

On October 1,1949, the People's Republic of China (PRC) was founded and an era of a new government began. China finally got rid of the imperialist meddling in its affairs and feudalistic and capitalistic oppression, and, for the first time since 1840, China could enjoy peace. The Chinese people could utilize their knowledge and wisdom to build up a modern country. The Communist Party and the government realized that, in order to achieve this goal, they had to unite all the peoples in China and involve them actively in the construction process. Certainly, the 3 million Catholics and those of other religions were included. Therefore, the new government made sure that religious freedom was protected as a constitutional right. In the 1954 Constitution, it stated clearly that all Chinese had freedom to engage in religious activities or not.

Yet, some pro-imperialist elements within the Catholic Church still insisted on an anti-communist and anti-people stance. After 1949, the Vatican refused to recognize the new government and continued its diplomatic relationship with Taiwan. Antonio Riberi tried to use his Pro-Nuncio title to control the Catholic Church in China. He sent to all the bishops in China the anti-Communism declarations the Pope had issued in 1947 and 1949 and asked them to pass on the message orally to their congregations: Chinese Catholics should not support Communism; should not read any magazine published after the liberation; should not get involved with any organization organized by the Party and the government, such as women's association, youth organization, scholars' association, workers' union, etc. The Catholic Church Affairs Progressive Association was found in 1948 under the leadership of Hua Li Zhu, and published many pamphlets to distribute among Catholics. They claimed that Theism and Atheism could not be reconciled. This influenced many

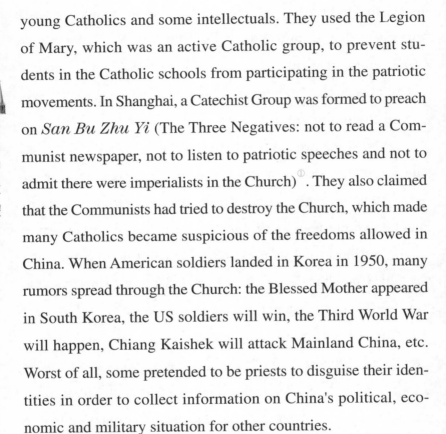

young Catholics and some intellectuals. They used the Legion of Mary, which was an active Catholic group, to prevent students in the Catholic schools from participating in the patriotic movements. In Shanghai, a Catechist Group was formed to preach on *San Bu Zhu Yi* (The Three Negatives: not to read a Communist newspaper, not to listen to patriotic speeches and not to admit there were imperialists in the Church)[①]. They also claimed that the Communists had tried to destroy the Church, which made many Catholics became suspicious of the freedoms allowed in China. When American soldiers landed in Korea in 1950, many rumors spread through the Church: the Blessed Mother appeared in South Korea, the US soldiers will win, the Third World War will happen, Chiang Kaishek will attack Mainland China, etc. Worst of all, some pretended to be priests to disguise their identities in order to collect information on China's political, economic and military situation for other countries.

The imperialisty presence and agitations within the Church influenced many Catholics in their understanding of Communism. They distrusted the Communist Party and were suspicious of the new society, causing them to be separated from others. Some even stood opposed the Party and government. Some activities of the Church went beyond the boundaries of religion,

① Gu Yu Lu, Zhong Guo Tian Zhu Jiao de Guo Qu he Xian Zai, Shanghai Social Science Institute press, 1989. p111

which prevented the Chinese Catholic from being part of the swelling Patriotic Movement. This very action interfered in the internal affairs of a country with its own sovereignty. Any country's constitution would want to stop this from happening.

2. CCP and local governments' attitude towards the Church

In dealing with the special historical background of the Catholic Church and the complicated social situation of China, the Communist Party and the Government put some efforts into keeping the Church under control. Focusing on the special character of the Catholic and Protestant churches in being foreign and their associations with foreign imperialism and colonialism, the government made some basic working policies and laws.

In November 1950, all the newspapers throughout China published a same article entitled 'The knowledge people should have on Catholicism and Protestantism'. This article looked at the way the imperialists had used religion to invade China. 'In China, there are two issues in dealing with Catholicism and Protestantism. One is its religiosity - it is a common faith that developed under social circumstances; the other is that the imperialists used it as a tool to invade China from the very beginning. We should understand these two issues and know the relationship and distinction so that we can deal with the problems accordingly. As a religious belief, those Patriotic Chinese do not think Catholicism and Protestantism should either be prohibited or rejected. Moreover, the materialists and religious people can and should be united in process of building up the motherland and attacking imperialism.'

The article called the church in the new China to rid itself of imperialist control. 'All those Catholics and Protestants who are patriotic should stand on the people's side to uncover the plots in which the imperialists use religion to spy on China. They should reject those people within the Church who still have connections with the imperialists. By doing this, the church can eventually be self-administrating, self-supporting and self-propagating. They should cut all ties with the imperialists and make the church a Chinese one.' [①]

Meanwhile, many people who knew religion and the Party members who were good at dealing with Christians were sent to religious affairs bureaus at all levels nationwide. Because of the efforts they made in uniting all the people, many Catholics realized that the government was truly protecting religious freedom to the benefit of all. The long suppressed patriotic feelings of Catholics could finally be expressed.

① Gu Yu Lu, Zhong Guo Tian Zhu Jiao de Guo Qu he Xian Zai, Shanghai Social Science Institute press, 1989. p114-115

3. Chinese Catholics' anti-imperialism and nationalism enhanced

On November 29th, 1950, Wang Liangzuo and 500 other Catholics from Guangyuan County, Sichuan Province issued a Three-Self's Patriotic Declaration, which indicated the beginning of the Anti-Imperialist Movement within the Church. This declaration called on all Chinese Catholics to cut any connections with the imperialists who tried to divide China in order to build up a church that was self-administering, self-supporting and self-propagating. This greatly influenced many Catholics. Many others, such as the priests and laity in Chongqing, Nanchang, Wuhan and Nanjing, issued similar declarations. In January 1950, Tianjin established a 'Progressive Planning Committee for the Tianjin Catholic Reform Movement'. This very action was highly praised and supported by the Communist Party and the government, as well the whole nation. By the end of January 1951, the number of the Catholics who supported this movement included 10 Bishops, Auxiliary Bishops and Vicar Generals, 186 priests, 46 seminarians and more than 400,000 lay people. They covered more than 53 regions, such as Kunming, Guilin, Guangzhou, Linchuang, Hangzhou, Baoding, Kaifeng, Qingdao, Zhang Jiakou, Jinan, Taiyuan, Tianshui,

© In September, 1950, the Sisters of Saint Joseph in Beijing Diocese were signing their signatures to protest the American Declaration on Nuclear Weapon

Fushun and Hainan. On January 17th 1951, many Catholics from northern China were invited by the Education Committee of the Government's Political Affairs Bureau to attend a meeting. Premier Zhou Enlai gave a talk in which he supported the Catholics' Patriotic Movement and encouraged all Catholics to build up a local Church.

While anti-imperialism sentiment and patriotism were spreading wide, Riberi and others began to distribute documents on the anti-patriotic movement through the Committee of China Catholic Affairs. They emphasized Catholicity and the universality of the Catholic Church beyond the boundaries of politics and nationalities. They criticized the people who started the patriotic movement as heretics who were disobeying doctrines and rules of the Church. Riberi wrote to all Chinese bishops and criticized the patriotic declaration made by Nanjing Catholics because they were being used by others. In April of 1951, he wrote another letter threatening that those who tried to overturn the Catholic authority either directly or indirectly would be disciplined by the Church. He also sent some of his own people to Beijing, Sichuan and other places to prevent Catholics from becoming part of the patriotic movement.

Riberi's actions appeared to be politically oriented, which amounted to interference in China's internal affairs and its autonomy. Many Catholics became angry with him and criticized his actions, and began demanding the government expel him. On September 4th 1951, the Nanjing Military Committee announced Riberi's expulsion. On June 6th 1951, the Shanghai Military Committee did away with the Committee of China Catholic Affairs formed by Hua Lizhu; on July 13th, the Tianjin Military Committee did away with the Legion of Mary formed by Ribeiri there in August 1948.

Facing the dramatically political and social changes in China, Pope Pius XII issued a pronouncement on January 18th 1952 describing the expulsion of the missionaries as religious persecution and urging Catholics to remain loyal to Rome. On

October 7th 1954, he again issued an encyclical *Ad Sinarum Gentem* in which he criticized the Chinese government for interfering with religious freedom, as well as criticizing the Three-Self-Movement. He threatened those Chinese Catholics who participated in Anti-Imperialism and Nationalism Movements with excommunication, while praising those who resisted participating in those movements.

This encyclical brought conflicts to the Chinese Catholic Church. Some lay Catholics were either excommunicated or denied communion for their actions against the clergy. Some clergy, under the leadership of Gong Pingmei, the bishop of Shanghai, were thrilled to hear about the encyclical and began to resist government control more aggressively. They called New China a 'Dark World' and the socialist policy as a 'Cat and Dog policy' (i.e. socially divisive). Their intention was to resist China's land reform program and destroy the socialist construction, as well as resisting the people's government's policy. On September 8th 1955, Gong Pingmei was arrested and his anti-revolutionary group was destroyed. Soon after, numerous cases, such as spying and anti-revolution activities in which Catholics were involved were discovered and many Catholics began to expose the activities of imperialists taking advantage of the Catholic

Church. Overall, there were more than one million Catholics involved in the patriotic movement.

As the patriotic movement became more aggressive, many cities established Catholic Patriotic Associations, such as Tangshan, Guanxhou, Zhengzhou, Nanjing, Beijing, Shanghai and Nanchang. By 1956, more than 200 local associations had been established. During the second meeting of the Chinese People's Political Consultative Committee in 1956, chaired by Xi Zhongxun, Secretary General of the State Council, some Catholic members proposed the establishment of the National Patriotic Association. In July, the Lay Chinese Catholic Patriotic Association Planning Committee held its first meeting in Beijing. This gained support from many Catholics, as well the highest Catholic clergy in China. In November 1956, Pi Sushi (1897-1978), archbishop of Shenyang, claimed that he would give all he had to support the proposal after learning of the work the planning committee had done.

4. Founding of the Patriotic Association

The first National Catholic representatives' Congress was held in Beijing from July 15th to August 2nd, 1957. This was the first meeting of such in the Chinese history. Among the 241 representatives, 11 were bishops, four Papal delegates, 58 Auxiliary and Assistant Bishops, 84 priests, one seminarian, nine nuns and 74 lay people. They came from 137 dioceses with a total Catholic population of three million. They discussed a new agenda for the Chinese Catholic Church, especially the Vatican's attitude toward China's politics and how Catholics should be more patriotic. Pi Sushi, the Bishop of Shenyang, said: 'The action that is derived from patriotism is the external expression of obeying God's Commandment. It is not sinful but an achievement, as well as a virtue. It should be encouraged rather than punished. Any kind of punishment that is unjust and invalid should not be accepted and therefore should be ignored. This is a matter of principle.' According to Catholic theology, he thought, the punishment should be imposed on evil rather than good; there was

◎ On August 26th, 1997, the celebration of the 40th anniversary of the Chinese Catholic Patriotic Association was held in the Hall of the People

no punishment if there was no sin; civil law needed submit to divine law. Therefore, being patriotic was not sinful.

On the last day of the meeting, the representatives unanimously passed the *Zhongguo Tianzhu Jiaoyou Ai Guo Yundong Qingkuang Ji Jin Hou Ren Wu* (Overview of the Past Patriotic activities of Catholic Laity of China and Future Tasks). They all agreed to establish a Chinese Catholic Patriotic Association (CCPA) and in the meantime, they passed the 'Chinese Catholic Laity Patriotic Association Constitution' (at the Second Congress in 1962, they changed the names to Chinese

Catholic Patriotic Association) and 'The Decision of the Chinese Catholic Laity Representatives'. The report declared: 'Patriotism is a citizen's divine obligation. A nation is made up of all the people and each one is part of the whole nation and everyone is an owner of the country. Whether a nation is at peace or in chaos is closely related to the actions of every citizen. In order to strengthen the nation and to secure the happiness of its people, the whole nation has the duty to safeguard and build up the motherland. We Catholics are part of the whole population and therefore, we cannot be denied our patriotism. On the other hand, there is another deeper meaning for our patriotism, which is that our nation's existence is from the power of God and patriotism is part of the Commandments.' The meeting's decision declared: 'For the good of the country and the future of he Catholic Church, our Chinese Catholic Church must change its colonial and semi-colonial status. The Church needs to be independent and be administered by our own Chinese clergy and laity. The Chinese Catholic Church will keep its relationship on a religious basis by obeying the Pope when dealing with Church doctrine on the premise of doing nothing against the benefit and dignity of China. However, the Chinese Catholic Church should cut off all political and economic relations and the church should resist when the Vatican tries to interfere in China's internal affairs and autonomy in the name of religion, as well as its anti-patriotic movement.'

In terms of the Chinese Patriotic Association, the meeting decided: 'The Patriotic Association is a lay group made up of Catholics who both love the Church and the nation. It is not an official church organization. Since the members of this association are either clergy or lay people, they should be aware of two aspects: first of all, the members belong to the One Holy and Catholic Church, and they should obey the Pope when dealing with Church doctrine; secondly, when the Vatican tries to protect American Imperialism and politically attacking the Soviet Union and Communism, as well as the socialism, we should draw a line by resisting interference in China affairs in the name of religion. We insist that we should cut off political and economic relations with the Vatican.' Meanwhile, the Constitution of the Patriotic Association stated: 'The Patriotic Association is made up of clergy and laity who both love the Church and the country. They are patriotic and should be actively involved with socialist construction and patriotic activities. They should protect world peace and assist the government to secure religious freedom.' The first congress elected Archbishop Pi Sushi as President of the Catholic Patriotic Association and Yang Shida, Li Boyu, Li Weiguang, Wang Wenchen, Zhao Zhensheng, Dong Wenlong, Li Depei, and Cao Daoshen as Vice Presidents. Li Junwu was elected Secretary General.

After the first national congress, the representatives went back to their home provinces and autonomic districts and cities to convey the congress messages and were all welcomed by the local people. Many provinces either established their own associations or formed a planning committee, such as those in Shanxi, Sichuan, Shandong, Jiangsu, Hebei, Henan, Fujian, Hubei, Zhenjiang and Shaanxi.

Obedience to the Pope in terms of doctrine and dogma and cutting off political and economic relations with the Vatican and resisting its interference with China's internal affairs in the name of religion, is called *Du Li Zi Zhu Zi Ban Jiao Hui* (the Three-Self's). The leaders of the Chinese Catholic Church declared on a number of occasions that, 'in order to glorify God and to save the souls of the people, the Church must follow the principle of being independent and autonomous. This is an historical development, which fits with the situation in China. This independent and autonomous church is only depicted in terms of political, economic, administrative and management aspects, not on the level of doctrine and dogma in any sense. The Catholic Church in China is the same as any other Catholic Church worldwide, which is one faith, one baptism. It is the same One, Holy Catholic and Apostolic Church. The bishops, priests, as well as the laity in China are the same as the bishops, priests and laity in any other country who pray for the Pope in their Masses and Prayers.' And, 'the Catholic Church in China is pure and true in terms of its faith. The reason why we emphasize the principle of independence and autonomy is not that we want to establish a new type of religion [because...] we still belong to the same Mystical Body of Christ as the Catholic Church in any other country in this world.'

The establishment of the Chinese Catholic Patriotic Association and 'Three-Self's' church not only united all Chinese Catholics under the patriotic flag, and changed the hostile status that the Catholic Church displayed towards China. This was recognized by everyone in China, and also helped the Church to advance its mission of evangelization. Since then, the Catholic Church in China has taken the route of both loving its Church and the nation. The Church develops well in socialist China.

5. The beginning of Self-Selection and Self-Consecration of Bishops

After the founding the New China in 1949, most of the foreign missionaries left. Some, who were against the new power in China, went to neighboring countries to await the outbreak of the Third World War so that they could return; others, who were involved in anti-government activities, were expelled from China. A few Chinese bishops misjudged China's political situation and left the country. This left only 20 or so bishops running 137 dioceses, which greatly affected Church activities and development.

In order to cope with this lack of bishops, on December 18 1957, Chengdu Diocese in Sichuan first decided to use the election process to elect Father Li Xiting as a bishop's candidate. This method was well accepted and adopted elsewhere. From January 1958 onward, many dioceses used a similar process and elected their own bishops, including Suzhou in Jiangsu Province, Yibin in Sichuan Province, Kunming in Yunnan Province, Jinan in Shandong Province; Guangzhou in Guangdong Province; Taiyuan in Shanxi Province, Nanjing in Jiangsu Province, Heze in Shandong Province, Hangzhou in Zhejiang Province; Yongnian, Yongping, Xiwanzi and Xuanhu in Hebei Province, and Yidu and Zhoucun in Shandong Province.

On March 18th and 19th 1958, Hankou Diocese and Wuchang Diocese in Hubei province elected Dong Guangqing and Yuan Wenhua as their respective bishops. According to the rules of the Church, the two dioceses notified the Roman Curia by telegram on March 24th and 29th. The Congregation of the Propagation of the Faith annulled the election in its replies on the 26th and 29th respectively, and reactivated the rule promulgated in 1951: any bishop, no matter what his status or the liturgy he uses, if he ordains any candidate bishop who is not nominated or accepted by the Holy See, will be excommunicated along with the candidate.

In the face of the severe shortage of bishops and the hostility that the Congregation of the Propagation of the Faith, the Catholic Church in China had no other choice but to protest. On April 9th, more than a thousand Catholics gathered in Wuhan to protest. On April 13th, during a solemn mass, Dong Guanqing and Yuan Wenhua were consecrated in Wuhan. Li Daonan, the bishop of Puqi Diocese, Hubei Province, was the main celebrant who was assisted by Bishop Wang Xueming of Suiyuan Diocese, Bishop Li Boyu of Zhouzhi Diocese and Bishop Yi Xuanhua of Xiangyang Diocese. There were 82 representatives from 23 provinces and cities who attended the celebration from Jilin, Gansu, Yunnan, Liaoning, Shaanxi, Shanxi, Henan, Hebei, Shandong, Anhui, Jiangsu, Zhejiang, Sichuan, Jiangxi, Hunan, Fujian, Guangdong, Guangxi, Guizhou, Mongolia, Beijing and Shanghai. The theory behind this action was the following: a) from the epistles, there were sayings about the election of church leaders who should be blameless (c.f. Timothy 3:1-2; Titus 1:7; 3:15.). b) the Council of Nicaea, which made the requirement for the presence of three bishops; c) the sayings of Pope Leo I that a bishop was meant to lead the people and be elected by the people.

Later, in Hebei Province, Bishop Zhao Zhensheng of Xianxian Diocese consecrated Wang Shouqian as Bishop of Yongnian Diocese, Pan Shaoqing Bishop of Xiwanzi, Chang Shouyi Bishop of Xuanhua and Lan Bolu Bishop of Yongping. In Shandong Province, Archbishop Pi Sushi consecrated Dong Wenlong as Bishop of Jinan Diocese, Li Mingyue Bishop of Heze, Jia Shanfu Bishop of Yidu and Zong Huaide Bishop of Zhoucun. Because of the needs of the Catholic Church in China, this self-selection and self-consecration movement spread rapidly. On June 29th 1958, Pope Pius XII issued an encyclical entitled Ad Apostolorum Principis in which he again criticized the Chinese government's policy on religion and the Chinese Catholic Patriotic Association. He also re-emphasized the papal power to name bishops, so that any bishops consecrated via self-selection and self-consecration process would not be legitimate.[①] China, however, did not pay much attention to this, because it considered the Roman Curia did not care much about the real needs of the Church in China and continued its anti-new government policy that could only be offensive to patriotic Chinese clergy and laity.

From 1958 to 1962, the Church in China consecrated more than 50 bishops. It was only because of the collaboration of these newly consecrated bishops and the older bishops that the evangelization of the Catholic Church could continue in socialist China.

① Ren Yan Li (editor), Zhong Guo Tian Zhu Jiao Ji Chu Zhi Shi, Religious culture press, 1999, p260

CHAPTER FOUR
THE CATHOLIC CHURCH IN CHINA AFTER THE REFORM

1. Reopening of the Catholic Church and its Development

The Cultural Revolution, which lasted from 1966 to 1976, was a horrible tragedy in China. The normal operation of the nation was seriously damaged and the people's daily lives were not secure. The Communist Party and the government's policies were criticized harshly. During those years, the Party and the government's official departments and offices that dealt with religious affairs were closed and religious sites either sealed or used for other purposes. Religious activities were stopped. After 1978, the Party and the government tried to restore religious ac-

◎ The largest Catholic Church in Beijing-Nantang which was built in 1650 with the money provided by the Qing government. It was damaged in 1976 when Tangshan had its earthquake. The Chinese government helped to repaire the damages

tivities and rebuild the churches, as well as in other areas in the nation where church buildings had previously been destroyed. The Party and the State Council issued a series of documents reaffirming religious freedom in China and disbursed a great sum of money to renovate the destroyed temples and churches in order for the people to have places to worship. They also rehabili- tated religious people who had been persecuted and mistreated during the Cultural Revolution. On July 16th 1980, the State Council passed a joint document 'Report on the Actualization of the Religious Policy on Religious Real Estate', which was submitted by the State Religious Affairs Bureau and the State Basic Construction Committee, Ministry of Foreign Affairs, Ministry of Finance, and State Department of City Construction, in which, they requested the restoration of ownership of all the religious buildings back to the respective religion, with compensation where such return was not possible.

The reopening of the Catholic Church was rather early. In 1973, when China was still in the midst of the Cultural Revolution, Premier Zhou Enlai allowed to the reopening of Nantang, located at Xuanwumen, for diplomatic relations' purposes. This was the only church where Mass could be celebrated in China. Most of churches were allowed to be reopened after 1979. On the Feast of the Assumption in 1980, there were solemn Masses at Nantang in Beijing and Xujiahui Church in Shanghai. The Catholic Church in China Magazine reported that about 3,000 Catholics attended the Mass at Nantang, among whom over 800 went to confession and 1,200 received Holy Communion. In Shanghai, though the church was still under renovation, there were more than 3,000 Catholics attending Mass. In the same year, Xikai Church in Tianjin finished its renovation before Christmas and resumed its normal religious activities, many other churches were also restored before Christmas, such as Hohhot in Inner Mongolia, Shenyang in Liaoning, Jinan in Shandong, Wuhan in Hubei and Chengdu in Sichuan. All these churches were occupied by either local government units or turned into residences during the Cultural Revolution.

In the 1990s, most of the Catholic Church's real estate was returned with the help of the local governments and church activities resumed as before. In order to meet the increasing needs of the Catholic Church, many dioceses nationwide had to expand their space. Certainly, some places received financial help from the local governments and others raised their own money to build churches. For instance, Liu He Cun in Taiyuan, Shanxi Province, where the church was destroyed during the Cultural Revolution, was rebuilt in 1985. The new Gothic style church cost 300,000 Yuan raised by the local Catholics. This church is 54 meters long and 22 meters wide with a capacity of 4,000 worshipers. Shenzhen in Guangdong Province was a small village for fishermen before the economic reforms turned it into a modern city. There was no Catholic church there before, but Saint Anthony's Church was under construction at the time of writing. This church covers 4,000 square meters, including offices, guesthouses, convent, rectory and an underground parting lot. The whole project cost more than 17,800,000 Yuan of which the

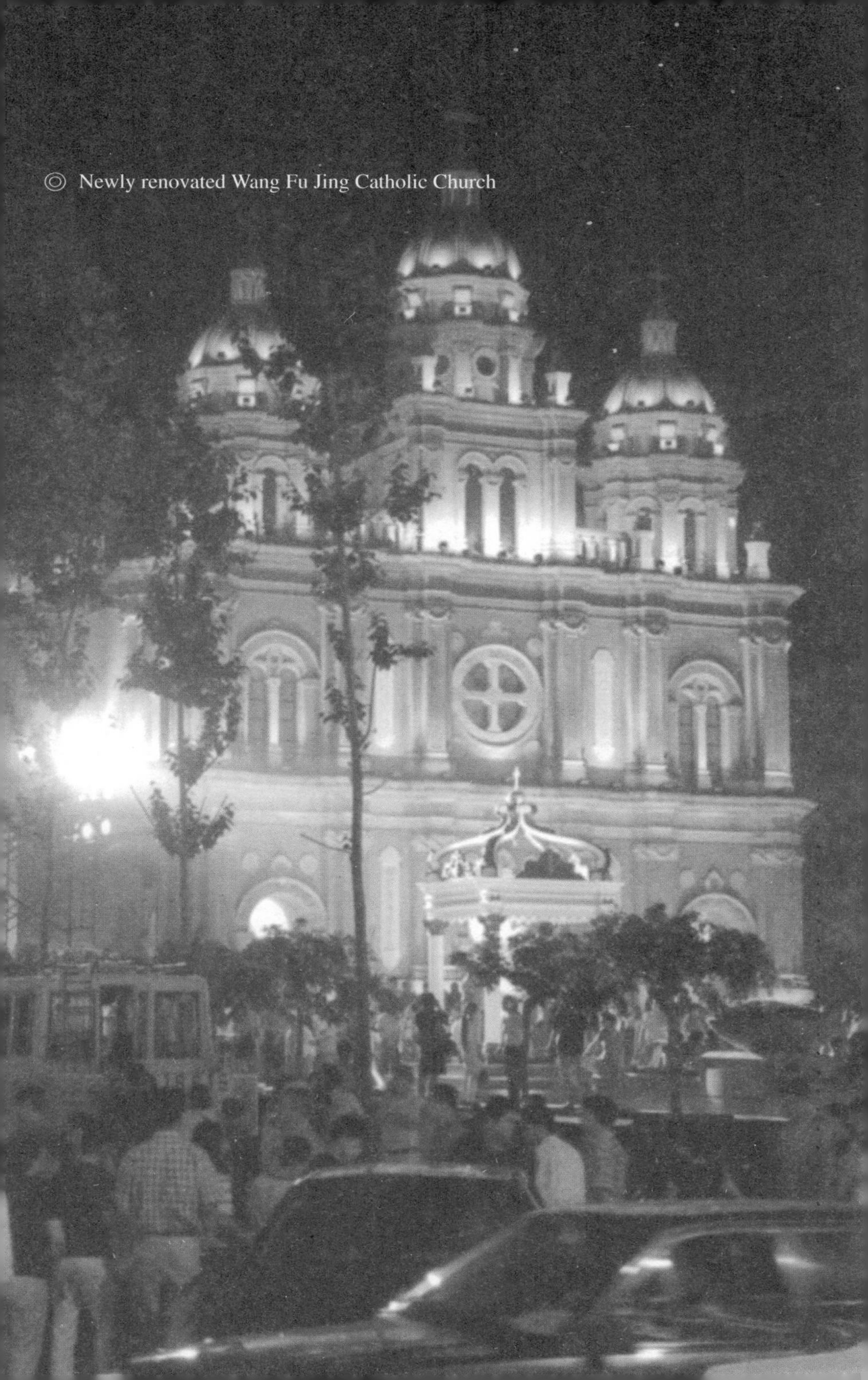

◎ Newly renovated Wang Fu Jing Catholic Church

government provided a subsidy of 1,000,000 Yuan and local Catholics raised the rest.

According to an incomplete statistics, by the year 2000, there were about 5,600 churches that had either been reopened or rebuilt. In the last 20-odd years, one church was reopened or undergoing rebuilding each day on average. In Shanghai alone, 108 churches were reopened, and the number of Catholics rose from three to five million, with 70,000 baptisms annually. There are more than 60 convents with 3,000 professed and 1,000 novitiates. Some three million bibles and other religious books have been published.

2. Establishment of Bishops' Conference of Catholic Church in China

On December 22nd, 1979, Fu Tienshan was consecrated as the bishop of Beijing and 25 participating bishops coming from seven different provinces, held a meeting to discuss church affairs. They thought a national organization was necessary for the Catholic Church in China to develop under the Three-Self's Principle, as well as to instruct the laity to understand doctrine and the catechisms. This organization could help solve various church matters and guide the clergy and laity to be faithful to both the Church and loyal to the nation, as well as, more importantly, glorifying God and saving souls. This proposal was well received by all the dioceses and a planning committee was formed with eight members, including Yang Gaojian, Li Depei, Zong Huaide, Wang Xueming, Tu Shihua and Fu Tieshan. When the Chinese Catholic Patriotic Association held its Third Representatives Congress on May 30th 1980, they also staged the First Chinese Catholic Representatives Congress. They agreed to establish the Bishops'

◎ The bishop of Zhang Jiashu (left), who was also a member of People's Political Consultative Conference, Vice-President of the Chinese Catholic Patriotic Association and Yang Gao Jian (right), who was a newly added member of the People's Political Consultative Conference and Vice Secretary General of the Chinese Catholic Patriotic Association. They were having a talk during the Fifth meeting of the People's Political Consultative Conference in 1979

Conference of the Catholic Church in China (BCCCC) and the Church Affairs Committee of Catholic Church in China. A constitution,'*Zhong Guo Tian Zhu Jiao Jiao Wu Zhangcheng*' (Constitution of Chinese Catholic Church Administrative Affairs) was approved. Its second article stated: 'This Committee is a national organization. Its principle is that the Bible which is the foundation of this committee. Inspired by the

Bible, this Committee inherits the traditional spirit of the founding of the Holy Church by Jesus and the tradition of the Apostles
to preach the Gospel, to advance the ministry of evangelization:
to glorify God and to save souls; to guide the laity to obey God's
Commandments; to insist on the principle of the Three-Self's
and a more democratic way to discuss important church matters
in order to strengthen the Catholic Church in China.' Article seven
stated: 'The members of BCCCC are the bishops of all the dioceses. Its tasks are: to study and interpret the Church's doctrine
and dogma, to share pastoral experiences and to have friendly
communication with overseas people'. The director of the Church
Affairs' Committee should also hold the presidency of the
BCCCC, and its Vice-Director should be Vice President. In September 1992, when the BCCCC held its fifth national meeting,
the church leaders suggested to reorganize the organization in
order to better utilize its capacity. At the meeting, they decided
to do away with the Church Affairs Committee of the Catholic
Church in China and to add separate committees under the
BCCCC covering Church Affairs, Seminary Education, Theological Studies, Foreign Affairs, Liturgy, Real Estate and Social
Services. In 1998, at the Sixth National Catholic Representatives Congress, they revised the constitution. Under the revisions,

article two stated: 'The BCCCC is the top organization dealing with Church Affairs. The Bible is its foundation, and, under the principle of the One, Holy, Catholic and Apostolic Church, this organization is to protect the treasure of faith and to strengthen church discipline. Under the guidance of the Holy Spirit, the BCCCC should preach the Gospel and expand the Church in China considering the complicated the situation of which the Three-Self's remain the guiding principle. Article three laid out the BCCCC's tasks: '1. Study and interpret Church doctrine and dogma; 2. Review and approve candidates for posts of diocesan bishop and, redefine and reorganize the dioceses; 3. Set up pastoral positions, write pastoral regulations for evangelical work; 4. Unite all clergy and laity to obey the national constitution and civil laws in order to maintain peace and unity so that the Father in Heaven can be glorified by our deeds and words; 5. Train clergy and those who devote themselves to God; 6. Represent Catholic Church in China publicly.'

The first president of BCCCC was Zhang Jiashu, the Bishop of Shanghai. After zhang's death in 1988, Zong Huaide, the Bishop of Jinan in Shandong, became the acting president and, in 1992, was elected president. After zong's death in 1997, Liu Yuan Ren, the bishop of Nanjing was elected to the presidency.

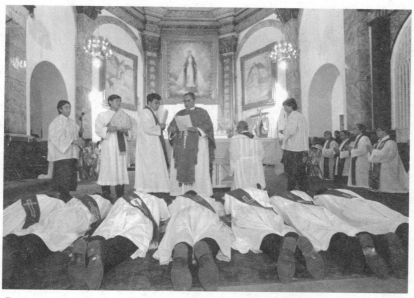

◎ Ordination of seven deacons (prostrating) at Beijing Xuanwumen Church was held on December 5th, 1993. Beijing Diocese has 33 priests now

The establishment of BCCCC indicated that the Catholic Church in China had entered a new era providing a good foundation for regularizing Church affairs and building up a local Catholic Church with special Chinese Characteristics.

First of all, in order to meet the needs of the new era, the Catholic Church began to promote actively and smoothly liturgical reform at the end of 1980s. In 1986, in the name of the Church Affairs Committee of the Catholic Church in China, a suggestion was made that, 'in order to conform to the national situation, to meet the needs of the new development, it is necessary for us to study the liturgy and make some adaptations. However, this study and adaptation process involves a huge amount of work and requires good leadership, organization and careful procedure. Therefore, before the Church Affairs Committee of Catholic Church in China and BCCCC come out with a unified decision on reform, every place needs to use Latin to celebrate Mass

© A Nun is teaching music

and there will be no exceptions. The local Church Affairs Committees need to strictly follow this instruction and resist anything contrary to it.' This was accepted and made effective. Shortly after that, the BCCCC and Church Affairs Committee of Catholic Church in China issued a joint statement entitled 'Additional Guide Lines on Celebrating the Sacraments for Clergy'. It stated: 'At the present time, the clergy must use the traditional liturgy and follow the rules. No one should make changes without permission from the BCCCC and the Church Affairs Committee of Catholic Church in China. On the other hand, the BCCCC granted Shanghai permission to reform the liturgy. Since 1989, Shanghai began to use Chinese to celebrate Mass. In the meantime, two priests were sent to the Philippines for liturgical training. In 1992, the BCCCC formed a special liturgy committee with Cai Tiyuan, the Bishop of Shangtou in Guangdong Province, as its director. Under the leadership of BCCCC, this committee was responsible for bringing together the necessary materials for the new liturgical reform: books for the Mass, rituals for the sacraments, music and prayer books. In collaboration with the Church Affairs Committee of Catholic Church in China, new guides were promulgated. These two committees were trying to study the needs of China in order to make the liturgy become more alive. In May, a group of 36 priests and two bishops from all over China gathered at the National Seminary in Beijing for liturgy training. The BCCCC invited two priests from Hong Kong to come as instructors. After the training sessions, all the dioceses started similar liturgy training in order that all should master the true meaning of the liturgy for the change to go smoothly. Now, all the parishes in China use Chinese to celebrate Mass.

Secondly, The territories of some dioceses were redefined accordingly. Prior to the founding of the New China, there were 137 dioceses. After many changes in the ensuing half-century, some dioceses were not in line with the country's administrative division and changes in the size of congregations in certain areas, and this motivated the BCCCC to make some alterations in order for the local churches to more easily manage church affairs. In November 1986, the BCCCC and the Church Affairs Committee of Catholic Church in China passed the 'Guidelines for defining Diocesan Territory' that stated: 'In order for the dioceses to more easily manage church affairs and considering the needs of pastoral ministry, all dioceses that are not in line with the government's city and district territories should readjust the diocesan lines after consulting with the local church affairs' committee and the neighboring dioceses.' For instance, the 11 original diocese in Hubei Province were combined into five new ones; in Shandong, the original four dioceses of: Yantai, Weihai, Yangu and Linqing, due to the small number of believers, were combined into two, Yantai and Liaocheng. In Guizhou province, the original Guiyang, Anlong and Shiqian dioceses were combined into one. As a result, the original 137 dioceses in China were reduced to 97.

Thirdly, normalizing the process of self-select and self-consecrating bishops. In 1986, the BCCCC and the Church Affairs Committee of Catholic Church in China passed the 'Guidelines for Selecting Bishops and Ordaining Priests'. Its first article stated: 'Those dioceses, where the needs of the pastoral ministry and the management of church affairs require the presence of bishops, should make a request to the Provincial Church Affairs' Committee. Once the request is granted, the diocesan priests and lay Catholic representatives should pray and ask the Holy Spirit to inspire them to nominate candidates and then go through a voting process. The one who receives over half of the votes is the selected one.' The second article stated: 'The bishop's candidate must be a priest who is devout and evangelical, patriotic and obedient to the laws of the country. He should be virtuous and knowledgeable, and one who also support the Three-Self's. He should care about the spiritual needs of his priests and be good at communicating with people and have their respect. He must be at least 30 years old and been ordained for at least five years. He should be priest with good looks and good health.' In May 1993, the BCCCC once again published a 'Guideline for Selecting Bishops', in which the age of the candidate was raised to 35 and it was made it clear that the vote had to be unanimous.

Meanwhile, the candidate had to submit the record of the voting process and his resume to the BCCCC for review. This guideline normalized the system and whole process of Episcopal ordination and offered a clearer requirement for the candidate. Since. 1958, when China began to implement the self-selection and self-consecration of bishops policy, 179 bishops had been consecrated, of whom 70 bishops are still alive at the time of writing.

3. Training of the Young Generation Clergy

During the 1930s and 1940s, under the help of the foreign missionaries, many Chinese dioceses opened schools and major and minor seminaries. After the founding of New China in 1949, many Catholic schools could not survive because of the blockage of the foreign economic support. The Political Affairs' Committee of the People's Republic of China took over the Catholic schools and made them part of the public educational system. All the seminaries were closed gradually because of lack of funds and the departure of foreign missionaries. In 1962, during the second meeting of the Chinese Catholic Patriotic Association, the representatives suggested to establish a national seminary managed only by Chinese clergy. A tentative decision was made to establish such a seminary and the Board of Trustees was formed. Later, because of Leftist interference leading to Cultural Revolution, the decision was not implemented.

At the beginning of the 1980s, as the church buildings were gradually returned to the Church, dioceses were faced with serious problem of the ageing clergy. Therefore, the idea of training a new generation of clergy resurfaced. At the third meeting of the Chinese Catholic Patriotic Association in 1980, along with

◎ Shanghai Sheshan Seminary

the First Chinese Catholic Representatives Congress, the 'Plan of Rebuilding the Chinese Catholic Seminary' was made. It declared: 'In order to preach the Gospel of Jesus and to continue the ministry of the Apostles, and to meet the needs of the Catholic Church in China, we need to have good priests and specialists in theology and philosophy. The meeting has decided to open a National Catholic Seminary and therefore has asked the Church Affairs Committee of Catholic Church in China to carry out the task.' Later, many dioceses thought that one national seminary would not be enough. Therefore, a decision was made that provincial and regional seminaries would be appropriate.

The first reopened seminary was the Shanghai Sheshan Seminary, recruiting students from Shanghai, Jiangsu, Zhejiang and Anhui provinces. This seminary officially opened on October 11,1982 with 34 seminarians. Its curriculum was a six-year system with Jin Luxian, who later became the bishop of Shanghai, as its first rector. Later, the churches in Shandong, Fujian and Jiangxi joined the Board of Trustees, so that Sheshan became a regional seminary for East China. It further expanded in 1985 and, the year 2000, it had trained over 200 young priests and there were 110 seminarians in five classes. It also oversaw two minor seminaries in Tailaiqiao and Suzhou.

Beijing Catholic Seminary, sponsored by the Beijing diocese, opened its doors to the public on November 2nd,1982 with only six seminarians. Currently, this seminary recruits students from Shanxi, Inner Mongolia and Tianjin. The curriculum covers four to six years. It rector is Fu Tieshan, the bishop of Beijing. This seminary has been moved three times. In 1999, the Beijing Municipal Government provided 15,000,000 Yuan to help the diocese buy a piece of land in Haidian District to build a modern

◎ Beijing National Catholic Seminary is a national seminary which is the highest educational institution to train priests

seminary with a constructed area of 6,700 square meters. By September 2000, this seminary had trained over 70 young priests.

The National Catholic Seminary in Beijing is the only national seminary sponsored by the BCCCC. It opened its doors in September 1983 offering a six-year curriculum. The first rector was Bishop Tu Shihua; followed by Bishop Zong Huaide, while the current rector is Bishop Liu Yuanren. The location of this seminary has also been moved a couple of times. Its current location is in Huangcun, Daxing District. Its goal is to be the highest Catholic educational school and theological study center in China. It will not only train excellent Chinese Clergy, but also be a center for theologians to carry out research. So far, eight classes have graduated and over 200 students ordained.

Zhongnan Seminary is a regional seminary in the mid-southern part of China. It recruits students from the six provinces of Henan, Hunan, Hubei, Guangdong, Guangxi and Hainan. This seminary was opened in October 1983 in the old major seminary for Hunan and Hubei provinces. Its rector is Bishop Dong Guangqing. Up to 1995, its 12 classes had produced about 300 graduates, of whom over 100 had been ordained.

According to statistics from the Seminary Education Committee, up to July 2000, there were 36 major and minor seminaries in China among whom 12 were major seminaries including one national seminary, which is Beijing National Catholic Seminary. There were five regional seminaries: Sheshan Seminary in Shanghai, Shenyang Seminary, Zhongnan Seminary in Wuhan, Sichuan Seminary in Chengdu and Xian Seminary. The provincial (municipal) seminaries were: Beijing Catholic Seminary, Holy Spirit Seminary in Shandong, Jilin Seminary, Inner Mongolia Seminary and Shanxi Seminary. There were altogether 1,900 students enrolled, and over 1,500 had been ordained, of which some have already become bishops.

In order to deal with China's weaknesses, Catholic seminaries decided to take a new route of 'going out and inviting in' which means sending students to study abroad and inviting foreign experts to come to teach. On the one hand, China sent some good young priests and seminarians to foreign countries, as well as Hong Kong to study. By 1998, it had sent more than 100 young priests and seminarians, nuns and lay people to the US, England, France, Germany, Italy, Belgium, the Philippines, Korea and Hong Kong. Those who have returned have already become very influential in the Church and the seminaries. On the other hand, once a while, seminaries invite overseas theologians and professors to teach temporarily. In the last twenty years, those invited theologians and professors have come from areas such as the US, Belgium, Korea, France and Canada, as well as from Hong Kong and Taiwan. Moreover, a group of 15 priests from seven major seminaries were sent to their counterparts in Belgium and France to study management in 1994 and in 1996, another 10 seminary professors were invited to go three seminaries in Korea for exchanges.

In addition, since the beginning of the 1990s, the Catholic Church in China began to hold short training courses on spirituality and pastoral ministry, publish reading materials on patriotic thought, send seminary rectors abroad for short-term training, hold training programs for the heads of convents and the master of the novitiate for sisters, seminary spiritual directors and lectures on retreat, spiritual direction and liturgy, etc. All these were done for the purpose of increasing the quality of theological education, spiritual formation and Chinese literature.

4. Promoting a More Democratic Church and Theological Studies

The People's Republic of China is a Socialist country under the leadership of the Communist Party. In dealing with all religions, the government adopted a policy to protect the religious freedom while requiring all religious activities to be limited within the descriptions set out in the Constitution, civil law and policies. The government is trying to encourage all religions to adapt the socialist system. The Catholic Church has learned from history that it can only survive when it conforms to the times and the environment. In China, specifically, it can only survive it matches the pace with the social development. The leaders of the Church have insisted that according to Vatican II's Ad Gentes Divinitus: 'The proper purpose of this missionary activity is evangelization, and the planting of the Church among those peoples and groups where it has not yet taken root' (#6). They believe that, 'the Gospel is a complete new rule that God has provided for humanity. Salvation is the everlasting mission and unchangeable. Yet, the spreading of the Gospel should be flexible. It needs to take consideration of different times, different countries, different races and their lifestyles and ideologies, as well as social systems. Adapting means not rewriting the Gospel or changing it, but interpreting it in a way that is acceptable to the local culture. The Holy Catholic Church was born in a slavery system inherent in feudalism and capitalism. The Gospel that Jesus Christ preached incorporated Jewish culture and what Paul preached was in line with Greek culture, while the Gospel in the West has always adapted to the local culture. The 2,000-year church history, actually, is a history of church readjustment to culture and changing times. History has shown us that the Church has to fit into society and only if the seed of the Gospel is accepted by the local environment and local historical cultural tradition can it take root and grow and bear fruit. The old China was a semi-feudalist and semi-colonial country. The Chinese Communist Party led the people and liberated China from this backward state and entered into a primitive state of a socialist system. It is a new question for the whole world to ponder, then, how to preach the Gospel in a socialist system.' (This is taken from Bishop Fu Tieshan's speech to the 6th National Catholic Representative Congress on January 17 1998). There is a belief that Catholics, both clergy and laity, have followed the example of the Apostle Paul, which is to 'be all for all peoples' during the early years after the founding of the People's Republic of China. History has proved that the choice for the Church in China to insist on the Three-Self's is the right one. 'After 40 years of pastoral work, we understand that the Holy Catholic Church can not only survive in a socialist system, but also can develop and grow in a healthy way Therefore, we must insist that the Catholics in China should love the nation and love the Church at the same time and should adapt to the socialist system (op.cit.).

On the other hand, the leaders of the Catholic Church in China also realized deeply that it was not enough to rely on past success, it has to keep up with the pace of time and enrich the content of the Three-Self's' policy. Only by doing this can the seed of the Gospel grow and bear fruits. One of the important elements is to promote a more democratic church and carry out theological studies.

This so-called Promoting a More Democratic Church does not involve a change in either doctrine or dogma. Its real purpose is how to encourage and organize the clergy and laity to participate in the management of church affairs. They should depend on themselves to discuss church matters in a more demo-

◎ Guangzhou diocesan Convent The first group of nuns were all from Catholic families

cratic way according to China's national environment. This is a trend of social management worldwide; this is also a request that the self-developing Chinese socialist society has for all communities in China. It is indeed the same as the Church's 'People of God' saying that all Christians have the duty and mission to preach the Gospel. By doing this, it helps the Church to make its management become more scientific so as to reduce human error. Most importantly; the Church can heed a wider spectrum of voices, especially, those from other sectors of society, which reflects the true needs of society. During the last four decades or so, the Church has had some successful experiences after many trials and practices. After the establishment of the CCPC, its mem-

bership was extended to all clergy and laity. All the local patriotic associations became a good model in terms of organizing
clergy and laity to participate in the management of church affairs. However, within the Catholic Church in China, there are
still some different opinions on promoting a more democratic
church as well as great differences in practice. All these things
need further research and comprehension.

The situation of the Catholic Church in China is quite different from the Church in Europe, though it has employed Saint
Thomas Aquinas' theological concepts. In order to establish a
Chinese theological system, delegates at the second Catholic Representatives' Congress in 1986 urged: 'Work hard in order to create an environment, to provide materials and to organize all the
capable people to study continuously the recent theological development. After organizing and editing all these materials, we
can develop a new theology which is workable in China.' Afterwards, a Theological Study Group was formed by the BCCCC
and had its first Theological Study Seminar in 1987. In the 1990s,
the BCCCC expanded the Theological Study Group into a Theological Study Committee with its own publication Theological
Studies, which comes out periodically. Many seminars were held
to discuss a variety of topics: Three-Self's, Church self-construc-

© The nuns from Guangzhou Diocese
were participation Church activities

tion, family planning, democratization etc., as well as theological discussion on the meanings of redemption and ecclesiology in a multi-system society.

On the occasion of the Christmas in 1999, the BCCCC sent out a pastoral letter Millennium Pastoral Letter to All Clergy and Laity in which, the themes of Promoting a More Democratic Church and Theological Studies were restated. The pastoral letter indicated its task as to build up the spirit of promoting a more democratic church, enhance the laity's understanding of church affairs and their participation. The letter also asked the people 'to move forward as the new era requires and change their opinions to respect and to lead all laity to participate in church affairs in order to work together to evangelize.' In terms of theological studies, it states: 'Enforcing theological studies and theological thoughts, study and research into the theories and methods suitable for pastoral work in China, advance the emergence of the Christian faith and Chinese culture so that a theory and guidance can be provided for our evangelization that will be able to adapt to the socialist teachings.'

5. Catholic Social Services

The majority of the Catholic clergy and laity believe, along with all their compatriots, that only the socialist system can make China a wealthy nation. Through increasing the productive powers and getting rid of the polarization of wealth, a socialist society can achieve its goal to make all wealthy. This is the only system that fits the Chinese situation and is not contradictory to Catholic social teaching. In the last century, especially in the last 20 or so years, the local churches and all the Catholic laity have participated in the socialistic development of the nation, and actively been involved in social beneficiary activities. According to the needs of society and the conditions of the local churches, many charitable organizations have been set up, such as medical centers, handicapped children center, social services, helping the poor and school dropouts, 'Hope' schools and other centers for special skills trainings, free medical checkups, helping areas affected by natural disaster and volunteer programs, etc. The church has extended a helping hand to those in need. These people's good words and deeds truly witnessed the love and virtue of all Christians.

In the summer of 1998, three rivers in China, the Changjiang, Neijiang and Songhuajiang, flooded many places. In order to

◎ Guangqi Kang Fu Center in Shanghai was funded by Caritas in Germany. It was finished on October 8th, 1988. This center is located in the middle of Sheshan with 34 beds to those post-surgery elderly patients

help the people in the disaster areas, the Catholic clergy and laity from 13 different provinces and autonomous cities, such as Beijing, Chongqing, Henan, Guangdong, Zhejiang and Jiangsu, collected more than 3,490,000 Yuan and 360,000 items of clothing for the relief services. In Hubei Province, the under the leadership of Bishop Tong Guangqing, the Catholic Church collected

15,000,000 Yuan. In 2001, when some areas in Inner Mongolia suffered snowstorms, the Beijing diocese provided medicine and food worth 150,000 Yuan. In terms of helping school dropouts to return to class, Shanghai diocese offered 1,000,000 Yuan to build four Hope Schools in Guangxi, Hubei, Hebei and Jiangxi provinces. Guangzhou Diocese responded to the call of the Women's Association to establish a Catholic Education Foundation to help dropouts in Gansu Province. Meanwhile, this foundation gives scholarship for excellent students.

In 20 years, the local churches collected a lot of money to erect hospitals, clinics, recovery centers, seniors' homes, kindergartens, handicapped children's orphanages, etc.. All these facilities showed the true nature of the Catholic Church in society. In Shenzhen, a Lay Catholic Volunteer Association was formed with about 100 members to visit nursing homes and orphanages periodically and bring the inmates money and gifts. They also have a free clinic for soldiers and those who have been widowed. In Liaoning diocese, in order to help the local people out of poverty, the church in Jinzhou established a scientific training center. They imported a good kind of young goose from France and invited experts to train the farmers in the right way to raise them, as well as other skills such as growing vegetables or fun-

◎ A newly wedded couple in front of Wang Fu Jing Catholic church on May 12th, 2001. More and more young people like to be married in the Church now

gus in greenhouses. This was welcome greatly because it helped the people materially.

Many dioceses took the advantage of having so many experts in foreign languages, professionals and medical experts; they established foreign language schools and evening schools for special trainings, which trained many good people for society. For instance, Wuhan diocese has a Kang Fu Medical College; Beijing diocese has its Xiangbo School; Shanghai diocese has Guangqi Computer School.

What the Catholic clergy and laity have contributed to society has been recognized by the government and accredited by people of all circles. According to the incomplete statistics, a couple of thousand Catholic clergy and laity have been recognized as good models for workers and pioneers by the nation, provinces, local cities or counties, some of whom were given the *Wu Yi Laodong Medal* (May First Labor's Medal); *San Ba Hongqi Shou* (March Third Red Flag Carrier); *Xing Changzheng Tuji Shou* (New Long March Shock Worker), and *Hang Ye Biaobing* (Professional Pacemaker) and others. Some villages and city districts, where there are many Catholics, were recognized as *Shuang Wenming Village* (Double Civilized Village) or *Wu Hao Jie Qu* (Five-Good street or district). For example, in Fujian Province, there are 15 villages where many Catholics live that have been recognized as Shuang Wenming Cun (Spiritual and Material Civilizations) by the local governments in the last ten years or so. There are over 3,000 Catholic families who have been recognized as either Wu Hao Jia Ting or Wen Ming Jia Ting; and more than 2,800 Catholics were recognized as professional pacemakers in the socialist construction process by provincial, city or county level governments.

Many local churches have educational, medical and other social services. The church people who dedicate themselves to these services through their loyalty, dedication, compassion and friendly attitude, have won much praise. On August 31st 2002, Beijing diocese held a grand meeting to honor those faithful participants in social services. The meeting was called *Beijing Tianzhujiao Wei Shoudu Liang Ge Wenming Jianshe Fuwu Biaozhang Hui* (A meeting was Held by Beijing Catholic Church to honor those who have contributed to the Construction of building up the two Civilizations). During the meeting, 115 people and 17 units were honored, among whom, there were clergy, faithful lay people who work in the patriotic associations, church workers and those who work at the Catholic printing presses; some of these people were retired, and some were still working. During the meeting, Bishop Fu Tieshan pointed out: 'Christ Jesus has already made clear for us our Catholic Church's position and the position of each and everyone of us, which is a position of service and dedication as a servant. Through our service for all people, for our nation, for society, we are witnessing for Christ. We are the light through which we earn the trust of society.' He continued: 'Serving the people, primarily is to serve the country and nation where we have been born and raised, and to be obedient to and in service of the highest interests of the country and for the benefit of the whole nation; it is also at the service of the capital's Liang Ge Wenming Jianshe (Material and Spiritual Civilizations). This is the grand service of the Catholic Church and the external expression of charity. As the Church in the capital, as a citizen and Catholic in the capital, we should be proud of ourselves because we have a double duty to be at the service of the capital and our Church. In order to fulfill out duties, we need to have a strong mission and zeal to position ourselves in the service of the 'Loving God and Loving Country' mission. We need to use our good words and deeds to beautify our environment, to purify our hearts, to vivify others and to sanctify our life.'

In addition, the clergy and laity of the Catholic Church are also actively involved in variety of social and political activities. More than 1,000 Catholic clergy and laity have been elected as members of the National People's Congress (NPC) and the Chinese People's Political Consultative Conference at national or local government' levels. Beijing's Bishop Fu Tieshan is a member of the Standing Committee of the NPC and Vice-Chairman of the Beijing Municipal Political Consultative Committee; Nanjing Bishop Liu Yuan Ren and Shanghai Bishop Jin Luxian are members of both the NPC and CPPCC. Meanwhile, the Catholic Church is an active member of the many committees: China Committee on Women and Children's Protection, China Charity Federation, China Red Cross, China Organization for the Prohibition of Chemical Weapons, Chinese Handicapped Association, China Association of Peace and Unity, China-International Communications Association, China Overseas Friendship Association, China-Foreign Peoples Friendship Association, China Anti-Sect Association, and China Committee on Religion and Peace.

6. Catholic Church's International Relations

In the last half-century, Sino-Vatican relations have not been normal since the Vatican refused to admit the legality of the government of the People's Republic of China. On one hand, the Vatican keeps its so-called diplomatic relations with Taiwan; on the other hand, it has not stopped its interference in China's affairs. In 1978, the Vatican gave 'dispensations' to China and 'simplified the orders of ordaining Chinese bishops and priests' through non-legal channels; inciting and supporting a small number of Catholics to resist the Communists, as well as socialism. This caused the development of a so-called 'underground power' within the Catholic Church in China. After the 1970s, a group of anti-China elements within the Vatican furthered enhanced their interference while China undergoing economic reform. On December 12, 1981, when Deng Xiaoping met with the Colombo, the Vice-Chairman of the Italian Catholic Democratic Party and Chairman of the Sino-Italy Cultural Exchange Association, he stressed: 'The first thing is the relationship between the Vatican

◎ From September 3rd, to 6th, 1985, King Constantine Beilun Saiyisuo Moshushu (sound) II visited Lanzhou, Shanghai and Guangzhou. This picture was taken in Guangzhou when he visited Sacred Heart Church

and Taiwan. If the Vatican solves this problem and admits that there is only one China, then China can establish diplomatic relations with the Vatican; secondly, the Vatican must respect the principle of the Three-Self's of the Catholic Church in China. This policy is written according the development of Chinese history, since, in the past, the imperialists used the church as an instrument to invade China. After the economic reform, although the Vatican indicated willingness to improve relations with Chinese government, and downgraded the ambassadorship in Taiwan symbolically, it has continued its support for the 'underground power', which it supported from the beginning. On October 1st 2000, despite opposition from Chinese government and the Church in China, the Vatican canonized some serious criminals in modern Chinese history, which really hurt Chinese people's feelings. This affected the normalization of relations.

The insistence on the principle of the Three-Self's of the Catholic Church in China is not to isolate the country from the universal church, and neither severs relations with other Catholic churches. Within the Vatican, the small group that is anti-socialist China still cannot stop the Catholic Church in China from communicating with other Catholics in the world. In the past half century, especially since the reform, the BCCCC and Chinese Catholic Patriotic Association and all dioceses in China have received tens of thousands of Catholic clergy and laity from all over the world, including some famous religious leaders and Catholic activists: Cardinal Etchegarcia from France, Cardinal Franz König from Austria, a delegation from the Asia Catholic Bishops' Conference, Cardinal Jaime Sin from the Philippines, and Mother Teresa from India, etc.

The Catholic Church in China has also been invited frequently to send delegations to visit many countries and their churches, which has enhanced the communication between China and other churches. On numerous occasions, Chinese delegations have visited countries such as Canada, Japan, the Philippines, Belgium, Hungary, Austria, France, North and South Korea, Malta,, Germany, Thailand, Singapore, Malaysia, Indonesia, the US, England and Switzerland.

The Catholic Church in China has also been actively participating in international meetings and activities organized by all religions. China has been striving to work with the whole world to further understanding and friendship and protect world peace, respect human dignity, achieve ecological balance and get rid of poverty, etc. In 1981, a joint delegation of the Catholic Church in China and the Chinese Protestant Church participated in a international theological seminary in Montreal, Canada. A total of 158 theologians from 25 countries from five continents participated. Bishop Tu Shihua, Bishop Fu Tieshan and Vicar General Wang Zicheng presented their papers *Du Li Zi Zhu Zi Ban Jiaohui Shi Women de Jingshen* (Principle of Three-Self's is our church's spirit); *Zhongguo Tianzhujiao Shenzhang Jiaoyou Wei Jidu Zuo Jianzhen* (Chinese clergy and laity are witnesses to Christ), *Cong Mangmu Fucong Dao Du Li Zi Zhu de Xing Ren Shi* (New Understanding of from Blind Obedience to Three-Self's). They tried to show, from both the theoretical and practical point of view, the correctness of why China insisted on the Three-Self's. From the beginning of the 1980s, the Catholic Church in China began to send delegation to participate in the World and Religion Peace Congress wherever it was held in the world. In January 1995, a group of 24 including young priests, nuns and lay representatives under the leadership of Father Chu Hanyu attended the tenth Catholic World Youth Day in Manila. In September 1998, Father Ma Yinglin, the Secretary General of the BCCCC, led a group to attend a 5th Seminar on a Chinese Bible held in Singapore. From August 21 to 28th 2000, the United Nations held a Millennium Religious Leaders Peace Congress which invited religious leaders from all the world to come to discuss the major issues the human race would face in the new century and their duties and responsibilities. A delegation from China, which was formed by the leaders of Buddhist, Taoist, Muslim, Catholic Church and Protestant Church, participated. The leader of the delegation was Fu Tieshan who was the President of Chinese Catholic Patriotic Association and the Bishop of Beijing diocese.

During the 6th Chinese Catholic Representatives Congress held in Beijing in January 1998, Bishop Fu Tieshan gave a working report on behalf of the BCCCC and the Chinese Catholic

Patriotic Association. He stated: 'As the further development of our economic reform, the friendly communications among the countries in the world are also enhanced. In recent years, because of the frequently friendly visits between China and other countries, many of our brothers and sisters in Christ have come to understand our Church in China. The misunderstandings are gradually disappearing and friendship beginning to be deepened. In the future, we continue to uphold the principle of "respecting each other, be equal and be friendly" when we communicate with any other country in the world. The Catholic Church in China is one part of the Universal Church and this church is willing to share the Christ's love with all other churches.'

图书在版编目（CIP）数据

中国天主教／晏可佳著；陈书杰译 . —北京：五洲传播出版社，2004.10

（中国宗教基本情况丛书）

ISBN 7-5085-0599-9

Ⅰ . 中 ... Ⅱ . ①晏 ... ②陈 ... Ⅲ . 罗马公教－基督教史－中国－英文 Ⅳ . B979.2

中国版本图书馆 CIP 数据核字（2004）第 101789 号

《中国天主教》

责任编辑：荆孝敏

编辑助理：蔡　程

图片提供：晏可佳　新华社摄影部等

设计承制：北京紫航文化艺术有限公司

翻　　译：陈书杰

《中国天主教》

五洲传播出版社

地址：中国北京北三环中路 31 号　邮编：100088

电话：82008174 网址：www.cicc.org.cn

开本：140 × 210　1/32　印张：5.5

2004 年 1 月第一版　印数 1-7000

ISBN 7-5085-0599-9／B · 45

定价：48.00 元